J. McT. E. McTAGGART

1907

J. McT. E. McTAGGART

BY

G. LOWES DICKINSON

With chapters by

BASIL WILLIAMS & S. V. KEELING

CAMBRIDGE

AT THE UNIVERSITY PRESS

1931

CAMBRIDGE
UNIVERSITY PRESS

University Printing House, Cambridge CB2 8BS, United Kingdom

Cambridge University Press is part of the University of Cambridge.

It furthers the University's mission by disseminating knowledge in the pursuit of
education, learning and research at the highest international levels of excellence.

www.cambridge.org
Information on this title: www.cambridge.org/9781107494916

First published 1931
First paperback edition 2015

A catalogue record for this publication is available from the British Library

ISBN 978-1-107-49491-6 Paperback

CONTENTS

ERRATA

page 24, line 24. *For* 'God' *read* 'good'.
page 92, line 27. *For* 'unaware' *read* 'aware'.
page 124, line 5. *For* 'a mystery' *read* 'mystery'.

INTRODUCTION

ALTHOUGH my name appears on the title-page of this Memoir, my part in composing it has been mainly confined to arrangement of the material. This was collected for the most part by Mr N. Wedd of King's College, Cambridge, with the assistance of Mrs McTaggart, and it is he who should have put it together. But ill-health compelled him to transfer the task—a very welcome one—to me. I knew McTaggart well, and in his and my earlier life read a great deal of philosophy with him. But my knowledge of his school life is derived from others, and from the time of the War onwards I saw little of him. I have relied, therefore, to a considerable extent on the reminiscences of others, and to all who have contributed these my own thanks and those of the reader are due. In particular my thanks are due to Mr S. V. Keeling, of University College, London, for the chapter which he has contributed on McTaggart's Metaphysics; to Professor Basil Williams, of Edinburgh, for the chapter on McTaggart's Friendships; to Sir Francis Younghusband for permission to quote from two of his books, and to Mr V. H. Mottram for the photograph which is reproduced

as a frontispiece. In addition to these reminiscences I have had access to some of McTaggart's
own letters. He was a voluminous correspondent,
but many of his letters have been lost or mislaid.
Professor Williams has a very complete collection
and he has allowed me to draw largely upon it.
McTaggart also left behind at his death many
volumes of the diary which he had kept from a
very early date; but through an unfortunate mis-
understanding all of these save one were destroyed.
That one volume deals with his second visit to
New Zealand, and I have drawn upon it in that
part of the book.

G. L. D.

Cambridge 1931

Note:—The reminiscence of McTaggart on pp. 66–68
was contributed by Mrs S. A. McDowall.

J. McT. E. McTAGGART

CHAPTER I
WEYBRIDGE AND CLIFTON

JOHN McTAGGART ELLIS McTAGGART was born on September 3rd, 1866, at 28 Norfolk Square, London. This date, September 3rd, as will be remembered, was the lucky day of Oliver Cromwell, and also the day of his death. McTaggart was fond of noting this fact. He was the eldest son of Francis Ellis, who later took the name McTaggart, and of Caroline Ellis, his cousin.[1]

The Ellis family can be traced back clearly to the

[1] Of the other children of this marriage two died in infancy, the fourth child, Margaret, married a doctor in New Zealand and died in childbirth. Her husband still lives (1931) and holds a post under the New Zealand Government. Norman, the fifth, contracted consumption, and it was for the sake of his health that Mrs McTaggart migrated with her family to New Zealand. Susan, the sixth, was born after her father's death. Like Jack and his father, she died of pericarditis, as also did some of Jack's aunts. It looks as though the disease may run in families.

fourteenth century. They were yeoman farmers
in Wiltshire, settled round Edington and Steeple
Ashton, where their monuments still stand. One of
them, John Ellis, left land to the monks of Edyn-
ton in 1422. They were farmers from generation
to generation until one Thomas Ellis (1730–1772)
broke away from the family tradition and became
a West Indian merchant. His wife was a Thornley,
also of Wiltshire. Their son, Thomas Flower Ellis
of Sevenoaks and Bedford Hill, Balham, married
also into a Wiltshire family, of the name of Danvers,
once famous in Stuart times, for one member was
created Earl of Danvers by Charles I, and another,
his brother, was one of the regicides. The Danvers
monuments are to be seen in Old Chelsea Church
and the house where the present Mrs McTaggart,
the wife of the philosopher, lives is built on ground
that was once the Danvers garden. This second
Thomas Flower Ellis, like his father, was a West
Indian merchant. His son (1823–1872), bearing
the same name, the grandfather of the subject of
this memoir, was a F.R.S., a Fellow of Trinity,
a man of some scientific attainment and a good
classical scholar. He was a Q.C., Recorder of
Leeds, and Attorney-General for the Duchy of Lan-
caster, and from 1834 to 1861 an official Reporter
of the Court of Queen's Bench.[1] He is best re-

[1] During the years 1834–1858 his fellow Reporter was Colin
Blackburn, afterwards Lord Blackburn, one of the first Lords of

membered now as the friend of the historian, Macaulay. He married Susan McTaggart, sister of Sir John McTaggart of Ardwell, Wigtonshire, whose brother, also John McTaggart, became later a rich man, and a baronet. Having no male issue, and desiring to found a family in the male line, he left money to his brother-in-law's second son, Francis Ellis, the father of the philosopher, on condition of his taking the name McTaggart. It was thus that Jack's surname became McTaggart instead of Ellis.

Francis McTaggart became a county court judge at the age of thirty-seven, and his memory still survives in East Anglia. It may be worth noting that his brothers and sisters showed traits which reappear in their nephew, the philosopher. Thus one had remarkable powers of mental arithmetic and kept a diary every day of his long life. Another was a good accountant. An aunt, a woman of many activities and accomplishments (including that of languages in which Jack never shone), was

Appeal in Ordinary, and a very eminent judge. There are eight volumes of these Law Reports known as Ellis and Blackburn. In 1858 Francis Ellis, the son of Thomas Flower Ellis and the father of the philosopher, was associated as Reporter with Thomas Flower Ellis and Blackburn, and the volume of Reports of the Court of Queen's Bench for that year is known as Ellis, Blackburn and Ellis. At the end of 1858 Blackburn ceased to be a Reporter, and the two Ellises, father and son, carried on the work for three years until the end of 1861. The Reports for those three years are known as Ellis and Ellis. These Queen's Bench Reports are, and always will remain, well known to the whole legal profession.

strongly opposed, as he was to be later, to the
repeal of the Contagious Diseases Acts, having observed from the records of her Rescue Societies that
the result had been an increase of disease. She,
like her nephew, had a passion for reading novels.
Of this whole family only two, Jack's father and
one of his uncles, had offspring.

A small packet of letters to Jack from his father
has been preserved. They are affectionate and
rather charming, describing, for example, hares
playing about in the early morning, fish jumping
out of the water to avoid a pike, rooks building
their nests, a water mill, farmyards and threshing.
One of these, dated 1870, still preserves in its
sheets a little bunch of dried heather. One is in
verse beginning:

> What a morning it was when as I drove through
>   the rain
> Punch wished himself back in his bedroom again.

Another contains a drawing of rabbits and par-
tridges, inscribed: "Some fathers and mothers,
some Jacks and Normans and Teddys enjoying
themselves in the sun". But the father died in 1870
when Jack was only four years old and it was his
mother who had most influence on his upbringing.
She, too, was an Ellis, the fifth daughter of the
youngest brother of Jack's grandfather, Thomas
Flower Ellis, and thus her husband's first cousin.

She was married to him on January 7th, 1864. Her father, Edward Chauncey Ellis, was a scholar of Trinity College, Cambridge, and Rector first of Dedham in Suffolk and then of Langham in Essex. Caroline was the fifth child of twelve. It is recorded that she was a professed agnostic all her life, a fact that was, no doubt, of importance in the history of Jack's opinions.

In the year 1872 Mrs McTaggart moved with her family to Weybridge where she remained until she emigrated to New Zealand in 1890. All through his life Jack was devoted to her, and this explains a curious and amusing anecdote contributed by a lady who was his playmate in Weybridge in those very early years. Jack it appears had been regaled with tales of the cannibalism of the Maories, and the idea that the qualities of one person could be transfused into another by the simple process of eating appealed to his childish imagination. Our informant records that he used to walk along the top of the garden wall

terrifying the baby me below on the lawn with descriptions of how he intended eating me for dinner, how I should be jointed, and how each joint would be cooked. I remember how distressed he was, when I reminded him of it later, to think he should have frightened me so unintentionally. One day in the woods on a picnic excursion someone suggested that we might get lost and wander for days, and what

should we live on? Jack said we would slay his mother
and devour her in pieces. Mrs McTaggart asked "But
what about drink?" and Jack replied "Oh, there is
always the water in your brain, you know". He was
devoted to his mother and I remember quite a scene
when Norman had been teasing her too much and
accidentally hurt her. Jack flew at him and seized
him by the throat with clenched teeth and the nearest
attempt at a fiendish expression he could manage. He
was a very eccentric little boy. He used to walk out
alone, walking sideways and swinging a stick and
holding long conversations with himself and was known
to the village children by the name of the "Loonie".

This curious gait was very familiar to all who knew
Jack in later life and was commonly attributed to
his habit of keeping close to a wall to avoid the
kicks of his school-fellows; but this note suggests
that it derived from an earlier date. And there is
reason to suppose that he had a slight curvature
of the spine.

More interesting, however, to us is the extra-
ordinarily early development of his bent towards
speculation. Thus, at the age of six, he is reported
to have remarked to one of his uncles, who was
endeavouring to console him for a death which he
felt, "we know nothing beyond the grave". Again,
a clergyman who knew him at this time in Weybridge describes him as running about on the
heath, suddenly stopping, running on, falling down,
starting off again, and again standing still, and

when he was asked what he was thinking of as he stood thus in meditation he replied that he was thinking about God. His brother, it is true, appears to have taken the view that he was only addressing a donkey which was tethered there, but brothers are usually profane.

At a very early age he was sent to a preparatory school at Weybridge. Here he was reported to have argued against the Apostles' Creed and even to have announced that he did not believe in God, with the consequence that he was incontinently removed. He was next sent to school at Caterham, where he seems to have been happier, though one supposes that the happiness must have been tempered, to judge from the following account given by one of his school-fellows:

At school he would play no games and football being compulsory he got out of it by lying down in the middle of the field and refusing to move. He used to spend hours drilling imaginary soldiers and I can see him walking up and down a wood-stack doing so. He also had a passion for sugar and I remember my father once putting a whole sugar loaf on his plate when he was staying with us as a joke. Jack gravely thanked him and ate the lot before he left! He never knew anything about his clothes and would wear anything, one buttoned and one lace boot for instance.... Of course we all looked on him as mad. He lived a life quite aloof and apart from other children, but he was always good natured and kind hearted, and in later years whenever I met him I liked him extremely and found him, of course, a most interesting companion. Jack as a boy was very sentimental in some ways and would always burst into tears and leave the room if a song called "The Little Tin Soldier" was sung.

Jack's career at Caterham was ended by the retirement of the proprietor in 1880 and his education was continued for another year by a private tutor, a Mr Ward, now Rector of Abingdon. He writes:

Jack was an affectionate but very odd boy. He was never boyish enough for games. He had begun reading Kant (and perhaps others) before 1880 and he spent his spare time on the common at Weybridge standing still or running jerkily for a few yards and then taking his hat off and declaiming something. He was very sensitive, especially about any animal life, as when his brother killed a fly, and he even disapproved of a flower being picked.

His early interest in philosophy is also testified to by Sir George Barnes, who tells us that when he was a young man at Weybridge, Jack, then aged thirteen, would meet him morning after morning at the railway station to tell him what he had been turning over in his mind. Kant in particular, he says, at that time was preoccupying the boy's mind.

Looking back over these fragmentary accounts of contemporaries we see a very unusual boy, incompetent for every boyish pursuit, incapable of

the rudiments of tidiness, preoccupied with philosophic problems, and already reading Kant, indifferent to public opinion, and pertinacious in the
pursuit of anyone who would discuss with him the
questions in which his mind was absorbed. This
first period of his life ended in January 1882 when
he went to Clifton.

The omens for his life at a public school were
certainly unpropitious. A letter summing up his
prospects has been preserved. It runs as follows:

What a queer boy Jack is, though I think some of
his tastes are merely affected. I don't mean hypo-
critically but unconsciously. At any rate I prophesy
rather a hard time for him at school. He will be
laughed at and humbugged for his oddities. Nor do
I think it will do him any harm if only he is not too
sensitive.

But following this passage is the wise and prescient
addition "though humbugged he will be respected
in a way. Boys recognise and reverence superior
knowledge".

Seldom, I suppose, has a boy so gifted and so
strange passed the portals of a public school. His
physical oddities combined with his outrageous
opinions made him from the beginning a marked
character. We have many accounts of this period
of his life. To begin with the physical side. It is
thus that Roger Fry, who was one of his intimate
friends at Clifton, describes his performances at

football. It will be observed that the situation was precisely the same as at Caterham.

He was sheltered by no indulgent doctor's certificate and duly appeared on the football field, but appeared only to stand, a limp, melancholy, asymmetrical figure, which showed no sign of awareness of what was expected of a player. To kick such a loafer into the scrummage was at once the duty and pleasure of an energetic back, but the figure merely sidled a few paces off and stood once more in dejected solitude. It was found that however often this process was repeated the result was always the same; no force could make McTaggart's body go through the rudimentary semblance of taking part in a game of football. The spectacle was altogether too demoralizing to be allowed and McTaggart got off all games for no more officially valid reason than that it was impossible to make him play them.

His incapacity was so complete and his refusal even to attempt to disguise it so absolute that "he was given the alternative of a five mile walk on the downs where he could philosophise with less interruption". This was a conspicuous triumph of mind over matter. But mind is not a popular thing in a public school and McTaggart's seemed likely to evoke an unusual measure of indignation. For not only was he very intelligent, but his opinions themselves outraged every standard of schoolboy decency. He was, to begin with, a republican and made no bones about it. There is a famous story

handed down by his contemporaries of which I will
cite the account given by Roger Fry.

Just before he came to school a madman had fired
a revolver at Queen Victoria's carriage in the streets
of Windsor. This attempt on the Queen's life was the
subject of conversation among the fags, when McTaggart, who was, of course, a sturdy republican, said
quite casually to his neighbour, "What a pity he
wasn't a better shot!" Schoolboy loyalty was in arms,
and the whole House shuddered as it heard tell of the
blasphemous utterance. The Fifth Form magnates
took the matter up and a trial was held. McTaggart
said that, of course, he must be allowed to cross-
examine the witnesses, and the judges, not quite knowing what this meant, agreed. But under his cross-
examination the witnesses began to break down and
contradict themselves so lamentably that the judges
decided that the trial must end at once and judgment,
i.e. condemnation, be uttered forthwith. The punishment was not, I think, very barbarous, and indeed
McTaggart's complete incapacity to resist any attack
made him an unsatisfactory butt for physical violence.

The punishment actually inflicted, I understand,
was running the gauntlet of knotted towels.

But there was something even worse than his
republicanism. He was more than an agnostic, he
was a materialist and an atheist. He did not apparently parade his atheism, for Roger Fry tells us
that he himself had never suspected it, and adds
that his reticence was due to

a scruple peculiarly typical of his character. He argued that being for the time an inmate of a Christian school he owed to it a debt of loyalty which forbade any criticism of its tenets. Indeed, his character was as precociously developed as his intellect, and loyalty to groups and institutions was one of its dominant traits; so that it was not until we came to occupy lodgings together at Cambridge that I learned that, before coming to Clifton, at the age of fourteen, he had absorbed and accepted the whole of Herbert Spencer's philosophy.

I record this piece of reminiscence which I have no doubt is correct, so far as Mr Fry is concerned. But I must add that in his diary Jack notes (September 11th, 1898) that he was unpopular at school because "we"—presumably his mother and his family—were not Christians. One is reminded of Shelley at Eton. But whatever Jack may have thought one may be assured that he did not parade his views with the passion of that great rebel. For the firmness of his opinions was accompanied, it would seem, even at this date, by his sense of solidarity with any institution to which he happened to belong. Moreover, his good nature, his freedom from all bitterness, combined with his almost sublime incapacity for all ordinary school avocations, ended by impressing the boys. Since he could not be bullied into conformity he must be made into an institution himself and thus digested without serious inconvenience to the standards of the community. Jack thus became a legend and a new cause for congratulation to the school. They had produced the limit of oddity.

"In short," Mr Fry writes, "by the time we left Clifton together McTaggart had made his peace with the community. There grew up in him not only a deep and lasting loyalty to the institution, but a romantic attachment to the whole Public School system and to all the patriotic emotions which it enshrines. His devotion to the school and my antagonism to Public School sentiment was indeed for many years one of the standing jokes between us to which each of us played up by exaggerating our differences. It was not until the war came that I realized how deep and compelling an emotion had hidden itself for all these years under the disguise of a caricature."

Probably scoring at cricket matches was what McTaggart most enjoyed at Clifton, but the sphere in which he specially excelled was the debating society. His name first appears there, so far as I can ascertain, in February 1883. The debates seem to have been conducted more or less on political lines, that is, there was a government represented by the President, Vice-President and Secretary, and an opposition headed by an appointed leader. The government, when defeated, seems to have offered its resignation, which was usually accepted. McTaggart was always in office, though the office was constantly changed from government to opposition. On looking through the records of the debates it is interesting to note that McTaggart was consistently on the radical side, supporting or opposing motions on which a few years later he would have taken the opposite view. For example, he defended the Irish, Egyptian and foreign policy of Gladstone's government in 1883; he approved Lord Ripon's policy in India; he argued that England ought at some time or other to give up her colonies, and he supported the disestablishment of the Church, the extension of the franchise both in England and in Ireland, and the abolition of the House of Lords. On the other hand his condemnation of Bradlaugh's exclusion from the House of Commons, of attempts to check intemperance by legislation, and of the agitation to suppress vivisection, he would, I think, at all times of his life have endorsed.

It is clear from the records that McTaggart's efforts raised to an unusually high point the prestige of the debating society and the numbers that attended it. Of that we have the testimony of so good a judge as Mr Whitley, afterwards Speaker of the House of Commons. He says:

His good nature was quickly appreciated and his study, rather than the library, became the place where good tips for a debate or an essay were to be obtained. He delighted to expound extreme doctrines in conversation and in school debates. The natural conservatism of the boys had a very healthy shaking.

Schoolboy debates became real live contests and masters thought it worth while to come and speak in opposition to the motions. It was a day of triumph when one of his propositions was carried by a majority of three in the largest house ever known. The worst adjective of those days was radical (bolshevik was yet in the dim future), but happily Clifton was a place where adjectives were not used to suppress genuine thought. This freedom may perhaps have had something to do with the development of the philosophic radical into the philosophic tory of later days.

In addition to taking this active part in the school debates, McTaggart wrote papers and poems in the *Cliftonian*. He was the author, for example, of a mature and admirable paper on John Stuart Mill, then one of his divinities, written in a singularly terse and lucid prose style. At this time he also wrote verse and took a school prize for a poem on Cromwell. This poem, I should say, is more remarkable for its maturity of thought than for any poetical excellence. Two sonnets are better, for that condensed form suited McTaggart's genius. Of them Canon Wilson, then Headmaster of Clifton, wrote:

I recollect seeing in the *Cliftonian* a remarkable sonnet and thinking that it was strangely like the thought of my late sermons, and when it occurred a second time I taxed him with it and he confessed, adding, I think, the very just remark that he thought a good sermon ought to have the quality of a sonnet, one poetical thought.

This sound principle he had applied in his own productions.

The position he had thus won against all odds at Clifton was enough in itself to account, in a man of Jack's temperament and character, for the hold the school had upon him, but I have not yet mentioned what was really the most important element in his life there. He formed a strong attachment for an older boy. So far as I know Jack has left no further record of this friendship, which lasted, like all his friendships, till his death; but the subject of it wrote in 1927 the following account of it:

About the end of 1882, or the beginning of 1883, someone told me that there was a boy in the Fifth Form who did not believe the book of Genesis. For some reason I determined to make his acquaintance and from that time we often took walks together after morning or afternoon chapel on Sundays. It occurs to me now, though it never entered my mind at the time, that he may have been grateful for this as at the time I was high in the Sixth while he was comparatively low in the School and in another House. I found him much better read than myself, and formed the highest opinion of his ability. The marvellous thing is that a boy of his type, who cannot have had a rosy time at first, should have come through his life at a public school with the greatest devotion to it. No one in the world could have seemed less likely to do so. I left Clifton two years before Jack, but we had become friends, and it was his reports from New Zealand that

1874

led me to come out here. I stayed with his mother when I arrived and Jack and I kept up a correspondence to the end.

This correspondence, unfortunately, no longer exists. But the brief account here cited may be supplemented by a note of Mr Whitley's:

Easy critics would have foretold the fate of McTaggart at a public school as that of a lonely and miserable soul. In fact, his Clifton friendships were to the end among the best of his life. His own loyalty brought out loyalty. His utter genuineness commanded first respect and then affection. Love is not in the vocabulary of schoolboys, but as it was the root of his philosophy so to one who knew him as man and boy, it is the only tribute to his great soul.[1]

Meantime Jack's intellectual eminence had made him known even beyond the bounds of Clifton. Dr Percival, then President of Trinity College, Oxford, wrote to his mother on hearing of his intention to go to Trinity College, Cambridge, to press the claims of Oxford, suggesting that the Fellows of his College might offer him an Exhibition or Scholarship on the showing of what he had written at Clifton. Had this arrangement been accepted it is interesting to speculate whether Jack would not have been as patriotic for the sister University as he became in fact for Cambridge, and as humorously contemptuous of the claims of Oxford.

[1] For love, as McTaggart experienced it, see below, p. 82.

Cambridge, however, prevailed and he went up to Trinity in the autumn of 1886. He took up there, as was to be expected, the study of philosophy, although Wilson had written to his mother an interesting letter urging a different course.

The line of study which I most desire him to take up is that of political economy in its larger aspects as the basis of social philosophy and finally of ethics. The students of this subject are few and it is the subject of the future. It will give him human interests, make him touch his fellow creatures at many points, and save him from becoming a professor in the more academic sense. I do not want to see a mind which is capable of dealing with facts and men losing itself in metaphysics, playing to a small audience somewhere in the clouds. I wish to see him in the thick of affairs.

It is pretty certain, I think, that if he had chosen, Jack had the ability to fulfil this programme, but the bent of his whole nature made it impossible. Evidently the impression he had made on Wilson was indelible, for after McTaggart's death he wrote of him as follows:

I often heard of him in the Forms below and knew that he was a remarkable person, and when he came into the Sixth I was greatly struck with his intelligence. From that time forward it is not too much to say that he attracted me more than any other boy in the school. I was certain that in him we had a first class genius, and the only question was how to educate him without spoiling him. I can say that his presence was a per-

petual stimulus to me. I never went into a lesson on
Plato, or Thucydides, or Demosthenes, or Juvenal, or
Persius without thinking of him. There were others as
keen, but he stimulated me to see all I could in the
thought as well as in the words of the writer. I knew
that it was an immense advantage to me. But the
most important fact of having so keen a critic was not
in my teaching in school but in my sermons. He and
a friend, Fry, used to walk on the downs, or meet
elsewhere, after my Sunday afternoon sermon and
discuss it, as I became aware from his own privately
made comments. He would come up when I was
alone on the downs, or even come to my study, and
say "Sir, may I say a word or two on something you
said a fortnight ago (or it might be more) in a sermon"
and then a passage would be accurately quoted and
very modestly questioned. The effect on me was very
great. There was no strain about it. He was perfectly
modest and was quite unaware that it was anything
unusual. It was invaluable to me to have such simple
but acute reasoning and that from one of my hearers.

McTaggart's own devotion to Clifton was even
greater than to Cambridge, and nothing gave him
so much pleasure as his election, at a later date,
on to the Governing Council of the school. His
feeling about Clifton is succinctly and charac-
teristically expressed in the following comment
made in later years on Mr Henry Newbolt's novel,
The Twynons.

I have been reading Henry Newbolt's new novel.
It is good but he ignores almost entirely the element

of romance about the place, or rather about the life. He says, in effect, that we were sensuous prigs, which is unquestionably true. But although a sensuous prig may not form a very romantic object in anybody else's life, yet his own life may be something to which the Morte d'Arthur is a Sunday-school picnic. And the business of an artist is to see people from inside.

If this remark be considered sympathetically in the light of what has been said in this chapter it will, I think, be felt to be a fitting summary of McTaggart's life at Clifton.

CHAPTER II

CAMBRIDGE AND
NEW ZEALAND

McTAGGART entered Trinity College, Cambridge, in the October term of 1885. I met
him, I think, for the first time in the
summer term of 1887, the first Jubilee year. I remember him then as a very thin young man with
large expressive eyes. He was at that time a
materialist of the John Stuart Mill school and I
remember that once when asked what matter was
he stamped his foot, like Dr Johnson, and replied
"That is matter". In the years that followed I saw
a good deal of him. He, Roger Fry, Nathaniel
Wedd and myself met weekly in a discussion
society. It was he who was the leader there, always
lucid, always witty and always with a kind of
throb of emotional life beating behind his deter-
minedly intellectual expositions. One used to come
away afterwards late at night and stroll down the
moonlit Backs of King's with a feeling as though
an apocalypse had opened. He was studying what
were then, and still are, called in Cambridge the
"Moral Sciences", and that meant that he gave

a great part of his time to metaphysics though other subjects were included. He also continued the debating activities for which he was famous at Clifton, and became Secretary and President of the Union. In this connection he says in a letter to a friend: "I have made a speech at the Union crammed with epigrams, that being what the house expects from me. Nothing is easier than to create the Cambridge Union epigram. The recipe is, take any truism and convert it contrariwise. Thus, say, that water kindles fire, or that refinement is the highest form of brutality, and the verdict of the Union is 'epigrammatic but cynical'". I remember in particular one brilliant debate in which he and Nathaniel Wedd were protagonists. McTaggart used then to wear a bit of blue ribbon hanging from his buttonhole which had been given him by somebody he cherished and which he made a point of openly displaying; and Wedd chid him for flaunting before the world "the blue ribbon of his intellectual superiority". Any chaff of himself always delighted McTaggart, for he was completely and unusually devoid of personal vanity or sensitiveness. We four, that is McTaggart, Wedd, Fry and myself, used at this time to row down the Thames from Lechlade to Oxford at the close of the summer term and those few days were a wonderful blend of fun and sentiment. McTaggart bubbled over all the time. He could not row, of course, but we made him do so. "Time, Bow" said the cox and McTaggart replied "Space". He read aloud or quoted Dickens, whom he knew almost by heart. The long stretches choked with rushes and reeds above Oxford; Abingdon, where we would pass the night and lie in the hay by the river; the wonderful wooded reach between Pangbourne and Maple Durham; the Hill at Streetley which we climbed at sunset; the locks with their roaring water; teas in riverside gardens; a moonlight night at Shipley; the splendid prospect of Windsor and ices in the famous tuck shop; it all lingers still in my mind after forty years, and the ghost of McTaggart rises up inspiring and enchanting it all, witty, absurd, sentimental, adorable. These trips continued for many years and once or twice we were accompanied by Ferdinand Schiller, McTaggart's greatest friend, whose pleasure, though not ours, was somewhat damped by his pained perception of the inadequacy of our bodies. McTaggart discoursing in the Society and McTaggart rowing down the river, that mainly is how I see him in my mind. But he was to be seen in many other aspects. He used, for example, to tricycle on an ancient and heavy machine and with astonishing endurance. His breakfasts and lunches were proverbial both for their brilliant conversation and their meagre fare. Every Sunday he used to watch the procession entering the University Church for the sermon. He rarely entered himself, but was watchful and critical of any lack of decorum in this official ceremony.

He took his Tripos in 1888, being placed in the First Class with Distinction in Metaphysics. The subjects of the Tripos in those days, besides metaphysics, were psychology, logic and methodology, moral and political philosophy and political economy. In the latter, then abstract, pseudo-science McTaggart had a thorough grounding and his opinions on economics throughout his life were determined by it. He was always a brilliant and doughty dialectician on the anti-socialist and free trade side.

Some passages from letters to a friend will show what Cambridge had already become to him:

"Unless I am physically or spiritually at Cambridge or Oxford", he wrote, "I have no religion, no keenness (I do not identify them) except by snatches. I must have been made for a don. As Wordsworth's verse ought to have said:

'One glimpse of mace, or cope, or hood
Can teach us more of man,
Of moral impulse and of God
Than all the sages can.'

The best part of the day is my walk round the Old Court between 12 and 1 with no one about but the cats and myself. I learn a good many things there, the chief one being that I am a damned sight happier than I deserve to be."

McTaggart took his degree in June 1888 and in the late summer of this same year he, Roger Fry and myself went out for a visit to Mrs Schiller, mother of Max and Ferdinand, who then had a house at Gersau on the Lake of Lucerne, with a tennis court and a bathing shed. The house is now the hotel Pension Fluhegg. This visit I look back upon as a kind of idyll of laughter, wit, romance, walks in the mountains, rowing on the lake, all presided over by the most human and humorous, wise and affectionate woman I ever had the privilege of meeting.

Ferdinand Schiller left for India shortly afterwards and on his first return in 1893 much the same party assembled at Gersau. In later years, whenever he came home, Jack and myself used to stay with him and his family somewhere in Switzerland. He must be thought of as one of the dearest and most constant of Jack's friends.

In 1891 McTaggart was made a Fellow of Trinity, and in the following year he paid his first visit to New Zealand, to which country his mother had removed with her family in 1890 for the sake of the health of one of her sons. She was established at Taranaki, near New Plymouth, in the North Island, and in that place was a neighbour of the Bird family, one of whom was later to become

McTaggart's wife. Margaret Elizabeth Bird, always called Daisy by her friends, was descended on the mother's side from the Kennedys, a Highland family from Inverness, and her father, who had migrated from Birmingham, was Supervisor of a large district in the colony. Jack's reputation had preceded him to New Plymouth, and his arrival there was anticipated by the young women with mingled apprehension and defiance. An Englishman! and worse a don! At the time when the formidable newcomer was expected Daisy happened to call on the McTaggart family. She found the house and grounds unoccupied, except for a quite unassuming figure seated on a chair in the garden. His general lack of everything that should distinguish the highbrow professor of legend made her quite unsuspicious of the stranger's identity. They quickly got into conversation which soon became so interesting to both as to make the whole afternoon pass in a flash until the return of the McTaggart family. Then a formal introduction was made and Daisy had to announce to her friends that the professor from England was not the supercilious prig that had been expected, but quite the opposite, and the rods which they had so carefully kept in pickle would have to be thrown away.

From the first, Jack's unassuming simplicity, his readiness to talk on all subjects with everyone, his

interest in the thoughts, amusements, occupations
and practical jokes of the community won him the
widest popularity, and this popularity was not confined to an exclusive set but extended to all classes,
and there is no doubt that it acted as a unifying
influence in bringing the little sets into which
colonial society was divided into closer touch with
one another. They could all meet on the common
ground of recognising that in Jack they had in
their midst someone whom they all of them understood, admired, and were amused at. For Jack was
a quaint figure in a society of farmers and rough-
riders, as a companion of robust, high-spirited,
farm hands, hard-bitten settlers and pioneers, and
boys and girls whose first impulse was to estimate
a man by his skill in games and the manliness of
his muscles. Jack had no skill in games; and
little practice in sitting a horse; it was only the
muscles of his mind that were massive and they
were not discerned at first sight. But Jack, here
as at home, was liable to demonstrate the mastery
of mind over matter by performing feats of physical
prowess that those who knew him best would have
thought impossible. He had already ridden a pony
in India, when he had stopped, on his route
to New Zealand, to visit Ferdinand Schiller.
Ferdinand took him for a riding tour up into the
hills and found the experience an anxious one.
"In Hegelian language", he writes, "the thesis was

Jack, the antithesis the pony, and the synthesis the hard iron ground." Jack, however, felt no anxiety, and was ready enough to resume his equestrian performances in New Zealand. His friends there set themselves to find him a mount such as might render even his combination of courage and incompetence harmless to the rider; and eventually a great friend, one Tom Bailey, a butcher by trade, owner of multiple shops, a stock-breeder, a colossally rich man, one at whom the *élite* of New Plymouth had been inclined to look askance, but who, like others of his class, recognised and admired Jack's qualities of head and heart and courage, succeeded in finding a horse which could be trusted to take charge of his rider under all circumstances, and on the back of Dottles Jack enjoyed daily rides, many expeditions and a delicious sense of athletic skill. In his letters at this time to Ferdinand Schiller, he records daily his equestrian feats with an obvious feeling of exquisite pleasure in having mastered a new branch of athletics.

Among his special friends must be mentioned in particular the Halcombs. Halcomb was a gentleman from England who had migrated for his health's sake and taken a sheep run in New Zealand. He never made good at the business and had a hard, struggling life. He and his sons and daughters became great friends with Jack. Their farm was situated in peculiarly beautiful scenery and Jack paid frequent and long visits to the house, taking part as best he could in the rough work of the farm, at least to the extent of rising early to take the farm hands their breakfast in the fields, performing with zest any tasks that were considered within the range of his competence, enjoying the apple-pie beds and the booby traps with which his services were repaid, and endeavouring to return such compliments in kind. His devotion to one of the sons in particular was very great and it was reciprocated. On one occasion when Jack's friendship was more strikingly demonstrated than usual, Queenie Halcomb looked at him and said, "Now, Jack, if you are ever as keen on any girl as you are on N. you will do as a husband". This forecast was amply fulfilled when later on Jack married Queenie Halcomb's great friend. Those were indeed among the happiest of the many happy days of Jack's life. He enjoyed the unusual sense or illusion of acquiring expertness in the use of his body, dexterity with his hands, physical endurance and athletic prowess, all the things that he lacked by nature and longed to possess, and at the same time the emotional atmosphere of the household and the magic of the scenery combined to stimulate his intellectual powers. He was always particularly sensitive to the influence of places and to the beauty of scenery.

Moonlight in particular had a remarkable fascina-
tion for him. He could rely almost to a certainty
on intellectual difficulties disappearing, or at least
being diminished, when he was within the aura of
certain physical surroundings. There was a place
at Church Rate Walk in Cambridge, near Caius
Cricket Ground, that played a part in solving
Jack's metaphysical problems. Certain spots on
the shore at Embleton, in Northumberland, had
a similar influence; but above all the Halcomb
house in New Zealand could be relied on to pro-
vide his intuition with the key to many of the
locked doors of philosophy.

But Jack's activities in New Zealand were not
confined to developing undreamt of physical powers
in himself and unlocking magic chambers of metaphysics. He also took part in the political and
social life of the community on its serious side.
The farmers and business men found that the professor had thought on more mundane matters than
metaphysics. They found that he had strong views,
for instance, on the question of free trade and protection. His views were different from those current in the colony. Generally the colonial was a
protectionist. Jack, though a conservative, was, as
we have seen, an ardent advocate of free trade;
and he was induced to expound his views in public.
The largest building, the Wesleyan Church in New
Plymouth, was hired for the occasion and from the

township and all the surrounding country the farmers poured in to hear the views of the newcomer whom they had now grown to respect. The place was packed. The lecture was a great success and the way in which Jack dealt with questions from the audience was even more successful.

This sketch of McTaggart's life, during his first visit to New Zealand, which is based on reminiscences contributed by his widow, may be supplemented by some extracts from letters to a friend.

New Plymouth in general regards me with awe. The only mitigating circumstance which renders life possible is that the boys regard me with contempt. If it were not for pillow fighting (or rather being fought with pillows) and metaphysics one's life would be a blasted sell, as the political prisoner said who was imprisoned for twenty years, and then mortally wounded by the prison being blown up with dynamite ("to prevent impertinent mistakes", as Sancho Panza says, "I may remark that this is a joke on the words 'sell' and 'cell'").

I have been out on my pony half a dozen times and off her once. Her name is Dottles. I enjoy the proceedings extremely, but I wish she were less deliberate. This afternoon she preferred walking to any other pace and although I had a beautiful raw-hide whip (I nearly wept at the absence of fags to benefit by it) I was unable to change her pace for the afternoon.

B. V. has gone back into the bush, having considerably flattered my vanity by making it very evident that he had liked being with me.

The flattery, he explains, was due to the fact that the boy cared for him more than he cared for the boy; and also that

he and I have not an interest, a characteristic, or a friend in common. So I must be fascinating *an sich*, as Hegel would say.

My letter has been interrupted at this point by having to go down to the town to order half a dozen of whisky, half a dozen of brandy, and half a dozen pints of champagne.

You considerably exaggerate the rusticity of this place. I would rather live here than in an English county town except for the daily papers and the greater possibility of getting away from an English town to somewhere worth living at. But the Society here is the better of the two I should think, and there is really no roughing it. The only difference is the scarcity o servants, and that is nothing to an Oxford or Cambridge man. I get more attendance here than I do at Trinity.

I have been bathing and riding every day. Last night there was an Assembly. I did not dress but went down to the hall and surveyed the gay and festive scene from the gallery. It was very pleasant to a lover of equality like myself to reflect that some of the gentlemen in evening dress were chemists and druggists, and others were cutting down trees in the bush at 6s. 6d. a day. That doesn't appeal to you, I fancy, but I always yearned for social equality, though I had no idea how much I liked it till I met it. I think some radicals would have had just the opposite experience.

The only thing I have to report this mail is that I have been spending a week in the country and enjoying myself very much. It was twenty miles off, and I rode over in 2 hr. 50 min., quite as if I had a body.

It was a pleasant place. With the elders (my host was a Charterhouse and Oriel man) I abused Gladstone in a highly satisfactory way. But I spent most of my time with the children—one girl and two boys ranging from fifteen to ten—who were pleased to make rather a hero of me, and to whom I took a great fancy. The eldest boy and I, especially, became great friends. We bathed and rode and boiled kettles for "billy" tea and drove unfortunate sheep to the slaughter, and collected edible fungus for the Chinese market—and I enjoyed myself very much.

A strange ideal sort of life—there literally wasn't a person about the farm, man or woman, who wasn't one of our own class. You haven't the same longings after social equality as I have so I suppose you won't appreciate what pleasure it all gave me. It was the thing best worth seeing (thing not person) that I have met and a good deal more interesting to my insane mind than Benares or the Himalayas. But we will talk it all over when I come back. Oh I am pining for a talk. I have not had one real one since the middle of March.

I must make haste and finish for N. is going to bring up two more boys this afternoon to make my acquaintance and he will be here soon. Everyone is in town for an Agricultural Show. Horses are exercising in crowds in our paddock, fourteen people are coming to afternoon tea, and the Halcomb's prize bull is to spend the night on our premises. It is desperately

exciting, I can assure you....I have no metaphysics
for you this week-end—they have been crowded out
by ladies' hacks, and Chamber spaniels and prize bulls,
and a careful and exhaustive comparison of house and
colonial lickings, which I am preparing for the Society
for the Promotion of Systematic Brutality. The state
of things in the colony is far better (i.e. more brutal)
than I had dared to hope!

From this first visit to New Zealand McTaggart
returned to Cambridge and Trinity for the October
term of 1893. He had been studying Hegel during
his absence and now continued the work, which
was to appear in 1896 under the title *Studies in the
Hegelian Dialectic*. In 1897 he was appointed to a
lectureship at Trinity which he continued to hold
until his retirement in 1923, and he must be
thought of henceforth, so far as Cambridge is concerned, as engaged in the writing of his books and
in teaching. Some account of the latter will be
given later. Meantime something may be said of
his other activities in the interval between his first
and second visits to New Zealand. Some of us had
started in those years what we called an Eranos
for the discussion of philosophical problems.[1] This
society was somewhat amateurish and perfunctory,
and I am not aware that any records of it have
been preserved. I have not even a list of the names

[1] This is not to be confounded with the more distinguished
society of the same name of which McTaggart later became a
member.

of the members; but I gather, from McTaggart's diary, that Professor Whitehead, the well-known mathematician and philosopher, was one of them, and so, at a later date, was Bertrand Russell. I do not even know when the society expired. Presumably it died in the end of inanition, but it continued for some years and was both stimulating and amusing. Jack, of course, was its principal inspiration.

During these same years he and I began reading philosophy together. My own remembrance of this is very curious. I cannot recall that we ever discussed any difficulties. McTaggart perhaps was too intelligent to require to do so and I, so far as I can remember, too inert and passive. I was interested in philosophy, as it seems to me, less for its intellectual problems than for its emotional values and was ready to wade through a good deal of more or less unintelligible ratiocination in order to get imaginative, or imaginary, inspiration. Like McTaggart, I was at that time a convinced idealist, but without McTaggart's determination to find a rational basis for the belief and certainly with a larger dose of natural pessimism. There was, however, another factor which entered into our method, or absence of method. McTaggart always wanted to get through, every day, so many pages. It is noticeable that, in the one volume of his diary which has been preserved, he constantly records exactly how many pages he had read of a book. Thus in December 1897 he writes: "Have done exactly all the work I meant to do this term, neither more nor less". This attitude of getting through the stuff is to be accounted for not only by Jack's conscientiousness, but by the fact that his philosophic reading had as its object not so much the discovery of a truth which he did not know, as the clearer ascertainment of the positions he had to refute if he was to establish the views in which he already believed. A characteristic entry, for example, is the following about William James's famous book:

1st April, 1898. Will to Believe, pp. 221–328, which finishes it, thank goodness. I never realised before how true Entweder Spinozismus oder keine Philosophie is, because I never saw how low a clever man could fall for want of Spinozism.

What he valued in Spinoza, besides the passion which made philosophy not only his intellectual occupation but his life, was his rigid and wholly abstract method. The great difference between the two philosophers was that whereas to McTaggart the important thing, indeed the only really existing thing, was individual minds, to Spinoza the Universal Mind was the ultimate reality.

It was at this time that McTaggart was writing the essay called the "Further Determination of the Absolute" which was privately printed in 1893 and has never been published in full. In this little essay he expresses more perfectly perhaps, and more freshly than anywhere else, the essence of his philosophic belief. I can still remember reading it aloud to Roger Fry, in his studio in Beaufort Street, with all the conviction of a sympathizer and all the admiration of a disciple. McTaggart writes of it, in a letter of August 1894 to Miss Bird in New Zealand, to whom he had sent it:

It has been shown to one or two people who are rather authorities (Caird of Glasgow and Bradley of Oxford) and they have been very kind and encouraging about it. I felt almost ashamed to write it at all. It was like turning one's heart inside out. However several people I think have cared enough for it to make me glad I wrote it. I hope though we shall meet before we get to heaven. In this life I hope, for if possible I am coming out to see my mother again. But if not in some other life? I can't help thinking it probable that people who meet once will meet often on the way up. That they should meet at all seems to show that they must be connected with the same part of the pattern of things, and if so they would probably often be working together. Very fanciful, no doubt, but more probable than thinking that it goes by chance, like sand grains in a heap, which is what one thinks in these scientific days, unless one thinks for oneself. All this reminds me of Browning. I was so glad you have read Rabbi Ben Ezra, and that you feel it is true. However hard life is, it can't feel worthless with that to look forward to—"fearless and unperplexed when I wage battle next. What weapons to select, what armour to endue". Have you read Evelyn Hope? I like that as much as anything Browning ever wrote.

In the same letter he writes:

One of my friends has got married and another engaged. Everyone always told me that my friendships would never outlast marriage. I never believe everybody, and in this case I was right; for the only result has been I think that we care for one another more than we did before. Anyway my beliefs have got two years' extra strength to them now. That is one comfort about being twenty-eight. The older one gets the freer one is from the fear that all one cares about will go as one grows up.

And again:

I have been buying you a book, Swinburne's *Midsummer Holiday*, but I am afraid it won't be in time for this mail. I send it you because I am so fond of the verses which begin "Oh delights of the headlands and beaches" and which end "Elect of the sea". I don't think anything I read ever helped me so much, it seems to put a meaning into the restlessness and dissatisfaction of all the things one does every day. There is something behind that he does not speak of, for the motion must be towards a rest where it will stop. Still it is very true I think and very beautiful.

From a second letter, also written to Miss Bird, I will cite the following passage which gives the other side of McTaggart's creed. Speaking of Tennyson's *In Memoriam* he says:

I don't think it's any good appealing, as he is rather

fond of doing, to the heart on questions of truth. After all there is only one way of getting at the truth and that is by proving it. All that talk about the heart only comes to saying "It must be true because we want it to be". Which is both false and rather cowardly.

He goes on, however, to show how certain, nevertheless, he is:

It is a wonderful poem. I wonder whether they have seen one another yet, or whether they will have to wait. Well, it would be worth waiting millions of years if one found the right people at the other end. I'm not frightened about any waiting—I am pretty sure that there is nothing in the universe strong enough to keep me away from some of my school friends in the long run.

Of external events during these years I do not know that there is very much to record. But one matter may be mentioned in which McTaggart took a very active part. There was a proposal to give to a Roman Catholic lodging-house, already established in Cambridge, the status of a public hostel. This would have meant its recognition as a quasi-college. McTaggart was opposed to this, on the general ground that any college or quasi-college should be open to all religions and all opinions. I agreed and so, as may be supposed, did many other people. The whole anti-catholic vote was easily mobilized on such an issue. There was an unusually large poll and both McTaggart and myself, I think, were a little dismayed both at those who sided with and those who sided against us. All the Liberals whom we respected were on the opposite side to ours. However, we marshalled our forces, provided gowns and carried our case by a large majority. McTaggart's note in his diary after the victory runs as follows:

I was very depressed after it was all over. I was more certain than ever that we were right but it was beastly to think of turning out N. and any of the others who really wanted to study; and still more miserable to think of having given Sidgwick his third defeat in 7 years. (12*th May*, 1898.)

Meantime Jack had become a public character and he describes with delight (for he was always ready to laugh at himself) a caricature which appeared in a Cambridge paper.

I am in the *Granta* this week as a rhinoceros in the book of Beasts:
"Philosopher, your head is all askew;
  Your gait is not majestic in the least;
  You ride three wheels, where other men ride two;
  Philosopher, you are a funny beast."
There's glory for you. (6*th Oct.* 1898.)

At the end of the Lent term 1898 we find him in London staying with Mr, afterwards Lord, Haldane. With him he visited the Synthetic Society, where were present among others Sir Alfred Lyall,

Dr Rashdall, Bishop Gore, Canon Scott-Holland, Mr George Wyndham and Mr Gerald Balfour. A paper was read on the existence of God, but McTaggart says nothing about that, or about the discussion. After leaving the society he went to the House of Commons with Mr Haldane and no doubt enjoyed the experience, in spite of his professed contempt for that institution. He spent the summer term of that year, 1898, at Cambridge, and left on June 12th for his second visit to New Zealand.

The voyage was uneventful (apparently Jack was never sea-sick) and he spent most of his time reading Hegel. He records, however, that he took the chair at a concert, and he was no doubt a good chairman, for he was accustomed to similar honours at Cambridge, and always took a strong line against any attempt to introduce on such occasions highbrow and classical music. On July 22nd he landed at Hobart where he records that "the art gallery contains the worst pictures in Euclidean space". On July 27th he reached New Plymouth and joined his mother at Taranaki on the 29th. He resumed immediately the intimacies and manner of life he had made and adopted in 1892. For this visit we have the daily entries in the one volume of his diary that has been preserved and on these principally I have relied, supplementing them by letters to his friends.

He resumed immediately his intimacy with N., and much that filled his mind and heart is illustrated by the following entries:

28*th Sept.* No work to speak of and no exercise. A typical day of the Unmittelbarkeit, Sehnsucht which forms an undercurrent to all my life in New Zealand. It was a good deal stronger than usual, partly I fancy because, as I think, my feeling for N. is growing stronger. Towards the evening I began to be happier and felt as if I understood things.

26*th Nov.* I rode with Queen to the G——s but could not go in as there was nothing to tie Cockie up with. Then for a walk round the farm thinking out my Hegel paper. Dinner was late and I looked at Egmont in the moonlight. It had been an absolutely perfect day. What with the moonlight, the Hegel and N. I was very ecstatic and the happiness was so intense as to be painful. The thing I felt most was how one would give up everything for love. Yea, though thou slay us, arise and let us die.

1*st March,* 1899. Up about 6, in the garden with N. in morning and afternoon. He began speaking of metaphysics, asking what the present tendencies were. I told him as much as I could. I said it was time for another great philosopher. "Perhaps it will be you" he said. And perhaps it will. Anyway it was pleasant to hear. I wanted to tell him that I did not believe in a personal God. I found that he thought he knew it already. I had told him that I had been brought up as a unitarian, and he thought it included that. He wasn't shocked but only said that it didn't make any difference about morality. A very jolly talk.

I have not had so many lately as he has not been working so much in the garden and that is the best place for them.

This friendship continued until N.'s death in 1919. On that occasion Jack writes:

I do not feel separated from N., not as much, I think, as I did during some years, when he was suffering from great depression and did not write to me. Since that we have been together again, and got much closer than before, and I do not feel less close since I heard of his death. I long to see him, but it is not a sad longing. I can wait, and I do feel it is only waiting.

This friendship, however, was by no means exclusive. Jack's never were. And in the same letter which has just been cited he writes:

Well, if my own life is narrow it gets wider by these things. You and M. and D. and N. (to take just those four) what different lives you lead, and yet "the lives that you lead are mine".

During all this period the scenery of New Zealand was making an extraordinary appeal to him. Thus, for example:

27th Oct. 1898. After dinner rode down to the Social. Started at 9 and reached home at 11.15. My first ride at night. The moon was almost full, and the last part of the way there were scarcely any clouds. One saw, to begin with, just the snows of Egmont floating in the sky. As one got nearer one saw the whole mountain and the ranges. It was very wonderful. I should have liked it to be longer.

14th Dec. 1898. N. and I were up by 3.30—before sunrise. The cows being in the park paddock, there was nothing but odd jobs, till the others got up. These two mornings have been very odd and delightful— getting up with the stars still there and going about with him before anyone else was up.... I helped Mrs Halcomb take in the washing, much to Queenie's delight, who longed for a kodak that she might send a copy to Mrs Sidgwick for the benefit of Newnham. They are much more willing to employ me on odd jobs than they used to be—partly no doubt because they know me better, but also partly because of the tremendous pressure of work just now. In the afternoon I was with N. in the kitchen garden, till he went for the cows.

8th Jan. 1899. Up at 4. Walk across Kochapo, I think. Rode down to Clements. N. caught me up there and we all three started for Ohsha Road. D. and N. were talking farming the first part of the time and rode in front. I rode behind, and thought how much luckier I was than the man in the Last Ride. But then, who is so happy as I am, I wonder! The first part of the ride is exquisite. The road is cut out on the side of a valley, with regular cliffs above, below and opposite. It is covered with exquisite bush. It is the first thing of the sort I have seen. We rode through The Gorge and back through the Greenwoods to a late lunch.... Dinner was at 8, milking having begun early. Afterwards we sang hymns.

On this visit, as on the former one, he gave

various lectures and addresses. Probably one of the proudest and happiest moments of his life was when he made a speech to the boys at the prize-giving of the New Plymouth High School.

16*th Dec.* 1898. I spoke for about 12 minutes. I began with the Empire and the race, and by way of justification fell back on the superiority of our schools in three points, games, schoolboy honour, and school patriotism. I ended by saying that if the five new peoples made their schools like the home ones it would show that the principle was of the essence of England—"they belong to the race, and the world—the world will belong to them". I was told (I was too excited to look) that the boys enjoyed it, especially the part about the games.

On April 9th he gave a lecture on Hegel:

I think Mr Halcomb and Queen liked it. I. M. and C. thought it necessary to come in, poor boys. I. and C. went partly to sleep. After this sang hymns.

It was during this visit that McTaggart's engagement and marriage took place. He had written frequently to Miss Bird after his return to England, and when he reached New Zealand in July he quickly got into touch with her. She came down to New Plymouth, and by January 1899 they were engaged. During the months that followed she must have been the centre of his life, and a note in his diary records the climax of his feeling.

9th July, 1899. The Saul feeling[1] came over me for
the first time in full strength since I have been engaged. The cloud that was coming up from Kei Pikin,
and the wind on the hills, and the light from the
dancing drawingroom windows, and F.'s trouble about
our engagement, these were things which I felt to be
nothing but love. I don't think I ever had it so strong
before, and it is very long since I had it. I was pro-
portionately pleased.

The wedding took place on August 5th, 1899, at
St Mary's Church, New Plymouth, and Jack thus
succinctly records it:

Walked with D. to the Church and was married.
I was not the least nervous, which rather surprised
me.

D. was his old Clifton friend, Dolby. Jack himself
would have liked a civil marriage, but Daisy's
mother insisted on the church ceremony. It was
performed by Archdeacon Govitt, then 92 years
old and a great friend of Jack's. McTaggart sailed
for England with his wife on October 12th: she
was sea-sick and he read Hegel. On September
28th they reached Plymouth, and after Jack had
shown her the sights of London and Cambridge,
and after the usual delays in finding a house, they
settled down to the life together which was only
to be terminated by his death.

----

[1] This "Saul" feeling is discussed in a later place (see p. 92).
He so called it after the close of Browning's poem of that name.

CHAPTER III

CAMBRIDGE 1899–1925

FROM the time of his marriage onward McTaggart's main object was to accomplish the task he had set himself of demonstrating by reason the truth which he already believed. Of that attempt something will be said later. Meantime it is essential to remember that, if he was a philosopher by nature and choice he was also a lover and a husband, a devoted son of Trinity and of Cambridge, a paradoxical wit, an enthusiastic epicure, and a whole-hearted British patriot. The combination is unusual, but it was his, and all these qualities were somehow reflected in his appearance, now becoming corpulent, his uncouth walk, his devotion to college and university business, and the pained expression which distorted his features when he heard a bad argument or an opinion which he considered heretical. Before his marriage he had made it clear to his wife that their union was not to interfere with his assiduous attendance at Trinity. He dined most nights at the College, did his work in his rooms there, and came home, as a rule, only for lunch and tea. Never,

I suppose, has a married Fellow permitted marriage to make so little difference to his collegiate life. Not many wives would have tolerated it; but Mrs McTaggart was as original as her husband, and as capable of conducting her own life. She had her work as he had his, for she took an active part in social movements in the town, and particularly in the work of assisting discharged prisoners. She had many friends of her own, both among men and women, and unlike many wives neither attempted nor desired to cut Jack off from his friends. The marriage, odd as it may have seemed in its external manifestations, was from beginning to end one of mutual comprehension and affection. Jack was not a man who expatiated much on his feelings, even in letters to his best friends; and the following extract from a letter congratulating one of these on his engagement may be taken as meaning a good deal more than it says:

I do hope it will be very happy indeed for you both. It is much better, I think, than one expects it to be beforehand—at least we have found it so.

Of this background, or foreground, of his life it is not necessary to say more; but it should never be forgotten by those who wish to understand him.

As we have already noticed, the life of a Don was thoroughly congenial to him. For this there were many reasons. He had, in the first place, a

1886

passion for system and routine, and a contempt for amateurs. College and University business claimed much both of his time and his devotion. Then he delighted in all corporate bodies, corrupt or otherwise, so long as they were not political, and especially in schools and universities. Further he was an enthusiastic pedant, one might say the poet of pedantry. These were the more superficial things that wedded him to the life of a Don. But also he found in Trinity and Cambridge the best possible home for his life's task. His lecturing and teaching bore upon the history and problems of philosophy, and though he lectured for many hours a week he had nevertheless time and leisure both in term and in vacation for his own original work. It was this work that kept him continually fresh and young. True, his inner spring of life ran in a sense underground, and, as he got older, was not always perceptible even to his pupils. But it was ever ready to spring for those who knew where to dig. As he never lost touch with his old friends, so he never ceased to make new ones. Neither class, nor age, nor occupation could keep him apart from congenial souls. He went through life knitting up relations which he believed to have originated in former existences, and to such a quest the differences referred to were external and indifferent.

He held his College Lectureship at Trinity from 1897 till 1925, and even after he resigned it continued to lecture six times a week on the general history of modern philosophy and the problems of philosophy. This lectureship was the only academic post he ever held at Cambridge. In the year 1902 he became a D.Litt. of the University, and in 1911 was made an honorary LL.D. of St Andrews. The only other outside honour I am aware of is that he was made a Fellow of the British Academy in 1906.

He took an active part in the business of Trinity, as is shown by the following account communicated by Mr H. McLeod Innes, a Fellow of that College:

It was after his return from New Zealand that McTaggart began to take a very active part in College affairs. It was a rather critical time, for the prolonged agricultural depression and the great fall in the value of tithe had seriously affected the College revenues, and for that as well as other reasons large changes had become necessary not only in the ordinary practice of the College but also in the Statutes of 1882, which had been made under the influence of an optimism not justified by events. McTaggart took a keen interest in the various questions which vexed the College then and during the rest of his life. He was elected to the College Council at the end of 1900 and remained a member of it from that time until 1921 except for an interval of five years from 1909 to 1914.

After 1921 he declined to stand again for election to the Council, but he took a full share in the discussions in connection with the Royal Commission and

its report and the Statutory Commission, and was an
active and useful member of the small working Committee which prepared the new statutes for considera-
tion by the College and submission to the University
Commissioners. It may be added that in earlier years
he frequently acted as one of the two assessors in the
College audit and in that capacity performed in the
most thorough and wholehearted way duties which
many have found tedious and irksome. In short for
a man who never held any administrative office in the
College he took an unusually large part in its business
to the end of his life.

That he was a most effective debater need hardly
be said. A College meeting attended by forty or fifty
Fellows is a difficult body to address, very critical and
sometimes even captious, the more so as it is commonly summoned not to initiate changes but to consider proposals on which a decision has already been
provisionally made. McTaggart's rapid, terse and lucid
method of making his point was much to the taste
of an audience which rounded periods always leave
cold, and his interventions were generally welcome
and often effective. But in the far heavier work of the
Council where discussion is informal and debating
qualities are of less importance his assistance was still
more valuable. There were of course some questions
which interested him much more than others: but he
was quite free from the common academic vice of
refusing to concern himself with things which did not
specially appeal to him. He always had a good grasp
of the business in hand, and though he not seldom
approached a question from an unusual angle his clear
and logical habit of mind and accuracy of expression

made his criticism useful even when his opinion did not prevail. His knowledge of College business and of the statutes and ordinances was almost unfailing. I did once find that he had overlooked a provision of the Statutes, and when I pointed it out he immediately disarmed me by saying "I am a worm and no man". But some time later he had his revenge at a College meeting when I made a similar mistake, which he instantly exposed, to the delight of the meeting.

To pass to McTaggart's teaching, it was at any rate in the earlier years singularly alert and stimulating. I append here two accounts which show how it affected able and enthusiastic pupils. The first is by Miss Stawell, now well known as a writer, then just fresh from Australia and full of every kind of enthusiasm. She speaks of him as giving her the impression of

one who had found the secret of the world and could have shown it to his generation. It was that impression that he made on me from the first and I have never lost it. And I know some of the reasons why he made it. It was because he had that rarest of all combinations, the keenest intellectual acumen and honesty combined with religious, poetic and mystical insight.

The lovable oddities of his appearance and ways, so like Dr Johnson, as we always said, only heightened this impression because they were bound up with the force of his personality. I can see him now, sitting askew on the edge of his chair, clutching the seat with both hands, his toes well turned in. I saw a photograph of Rodin's "Penseur" for the first time one day after he had come to see us. And I said the position of the feet and the figure struck me as odd for a philosopher. "Well", answered ——, "it is just the way your friend McTaggart sits."

Here, one felt, was a man who would never be led to speak smooth things about the universe, to flatter creation, for ease to himself or the pleasure of a sentimental pose. The last thing one could imagine his being was sentimental. Nothing was more characteristic of him than the remark in one of his writings, "A mysticism that ignores the claims of the understanding is doomed". But I think I always felt, even from the beginning, that the supreme thing for him *was* the mysticism. Only I come back to this: his mind at once appealed to me because the two things, mysticism and understanding, were obviously, for him, not merely not incompatible but vitally united. And along with this went his ready irresistible humour. I remember Theodore Llewellyn Davies asking me if I didn't notice, when he was lecturing on Hegel, that the harder and more abstruse the dialectic became, the more lambent and electric grew McTaggart's humour. I certainly did!

It was through his lectures on Hegel that I first came to know him, in the Spring Term of 1893 at Cambridge. I was twenty-four and I suppose he was only a few years older.[1] He came up three times a week to Newnham just to lecture to three young women on Hegel, and he did this because, he said, he would do a great deal for Hegel. I don't know if he had any notes, I think not: at any rate he spoke,

---

[1] He was in his twenty-seventh year.

sitting at a little table, the rest of us at the three sides, without the least hesitation and with most astonishing clearness. I could take notes quickly then, and I scribbled so fast that I think I got almost everything down. But not the impromptu answers to my halting questions: there were not many of these, for I was too shy to put questions, but I remember pretty well even now most of the answers. Two of them were very typical. One because of the quickness with which he understood the difficulties of a beginner. He had been trying to explain to us the Hegelian transition from the conception of mere undifferentiated "Being" to the conception of mere "Nothing". This was entirely new to me and I said—in response to his asking if he had made it at all clear—"Do you mean that the second conception is *inferred* from the first, or that it really is only another way of stating the first?"— something like that, I can't remember the exact phrasing. But I shall always remember the eager luminous look that came into his eyes, irradiating the whole queer face, and the way he said, "Well, the answer to that is that the precise relation of the two conceptions is beyond the scope of language, at least of my language. I can only say that the relation is such that if you think the one you find you are thinking the other". I wish I could make clear his intense desire to show what he saw himself and his delight if the difficulties of his students were the right *kind* of difficulties, the difficulties that showed one was more or less aware of the peaks and the precipices. The other answer was, I felt, a neat example of his humour. He was trying to show us that the more living a unity, the more differences it involved. This again was pretty much an entirely new idea to me: I am sure I gasped and I believe I said something which showed I was all abroad. He saw and went on: "Well, you could hardly say that a pin-point was as much of a living unity as a man. If there were only two pin-points in the universe, all you could say of the differences between them would be that one was one and the other was the other. But if you were asked the difference between Kant and Hegel it wouldn't be much of an answer to repeat 'that one was one and the other was the other'".

Years after I compared my old notes with McTaggart's own books on the Dialectic and it was fascinating to observe the changes and to watch how his mind had moved, how ready he was to give up minor points while keeping fast hold of what to him was the pith of the matter. He has always made credible to me how this might lie in the Dialectic itself, I don't mean in all its details—no doubt in detail it is full of lapses and flaws and it is pretty evident, I think, from the changes I spoke of that McTaggart himself would have admitted that—but he has made me feel that the central principle might be the right one, the principle that an all-inclusive harmony somehow underlies every bit of experience and that a reference to it is somehow involved in every statement, however meagre, and could be made explicit if that statement was coherently thought out. I am using my own words—McTaggart might have altered them—but it is to him I owe these ideas and always he made them seem not only inspiring but *true*. I remember his saying of a book by Caird on Hegel, "It's a fine book and one you ought to read, very inspiring and all that, only he doesn't bring out clearly enough why the whole thing should be true, and that, in the end, is what we are after".

At the same time, for all the importance—in one sense the supreme importance—that he attached to metaphysical analysis, he saw the importance of other things. When I said to him once, "'where there is no vision the people perish', and to most people metaphysical analysis can nourish no vision without something else to take the place of outworn religious dogma", he answered very gravely, "Yes, I know: it's the tragedy of metaphysics". But tragedy was never the last word with him because his own vision was so vital and enduring. And this leads me back to the profoundest thing about him. I think I first became aware of it—(and it is characteristic of him that it should have been so)—when he was lecturing on this very point of the reference to an ultimate all-harmonious reality involved in any statement. He said something like this: "In the end the mainspring of the Dialectic is the fact that this Reality is there all the time; the human mind in thinking-out its own thoughts is not operating alone".

It has been said that the great religions of the world could be divided into the religions of Time and the religions of Eternity. Well, I think McTaggart's religion, like Goethe's, though he was exceedingly different from Goethe, was one of both. "Poetry and common-sense", he wrote somewhere, "are ill to quarrel with", and I remember asking him once if he didn't think that most philosophers flouted them and were themselves extremely uncritical in assuming that the relation of the future to the present was the same as the relation of the past, except for the mere difference of direction, and the future in no way more valuable. He would not be drawn on this occasion. He said—and this also was characteristic of him—that he didn't feel his thoughts sufficiently clearly arranged to discuss it. I felt rather snubbed, for certainly my own were not, but when I read a later book of his on the subject I saw that he did think there was a real significance in the conviction of poetry and common-sense that it was the Future that mattered most and that progress in Time was the symbol of the eternal perfection.

It was like him also and like his human warmth of feeling to have a deep desire for and an intellectual belief in immortality as the place for the completion of the imperfect loves we know of here. He used to laugh at me a good deal for my enthusiasms. "What a pity it is Melian won't drink wine", he said to his wife one day when I was lunching there, "it really is too bad of her." This quite seriously; then, cheering up, "But never mind! She's always drunk without it". This was all very well, I could have retorted, when he knew he liked to be quietly intoxicated himself. Sometimes he admitted as much. I mentioned one day that you often mocked at me for wanting to eat my cake and have it too, but that I considered with a proper cake this could easily be done. "O, that's nothing!" McTaggart answered gravely and eagerly, "With a *proper* cake the more you eat it the bigger it gets."

The other account refers to a later period and is sent to me by Professor L. G. Struthers.

"I will try", he says, "to describe the relations of an ordinary pupil to him as pupil to teacher. I say an ordinary pupil, because possibly in the case of highly gifted pupils his interest in them as persons may have been aroused a great deal more, and this may have made a lot of difference. But this I did not witness and know nothing about.

I suppose the first impression was one of extreme kindliness unaccompanied by any touch of surface urbanity. I mean to say, he did not smile or attempt to put you at your ease by any arts whatever; his manner of speaking was dry and terse; he appeared to care nothing for your feelings or past history or tastes or anything like that; you knew at once that none of that was to the point—it would not be asked about and had better not be spoken about; and yet you got an impression of utter benevolence, of readiness to tell all and do all for your benefit. I think I might say that you were treated from the first moment as a mind and solely as a mind, a mind seeking directions about lectures, advice about the Tripos, and, above all, general guidance in philosophy. And you found out fairly soon that it was as a mind that you had to justify yourself and stand up before him—as a mind occupied with philosophical problems. Ideals and aspirations tinged with emotion, smartness of expression, wit, irrelevant knowledge however impressive or interesting in itself, received as such no sort of recognition from him: the only thing he would consider or allow you to consider was whether the thing said was intellectually sound. You had to show that it was good in logic in itself, so far as it went, and then that it was not inconsistent with anything else that you might have to admit, or had, perhaps unwittingly, already admitted. All this was done by rapid and short remarks and questions on McTaggart's part—

sometimes incredibly rapid and exasperatingly short. His mind seemed to be ready at once for everything, prepared with objections, ready in the tersest and liveliest form for use, to every possible unsound argument. But your rewards were that McTaggart, never showing scorn or impatience, but often relish, would infallibly keep the ball rolling as long as you were willing or able to do so; everything depended on your own efforts; so long as you were game he was; and this was intensely stimulating even when he showed you at the end, as usually happened at such discussions, that you couldn't hold the opinion you were trying to hold. And the other great reward that you occasionally enjoyed was when you came through in an argument and met him by fair means in a just and firm sympathetic encounter in some belief or (still more rarely) some emotion. Then, when all was justified, he would be prepared to enjoy wit or moral earnestness or satire or cleverness or generous emotion or any other decoration, and the pupil would feel then the richness of his nature. For in fact he was brimming over with all those qualities himself, though moral earnestness was seldom evident except when he spoke about love.

I disagree a little with Broad's suggestion in his memoir[1] that McTaggart was apt to "score off" a questioner by a single brief answer instead of trying to find out what, if anything, lay behind the question. I don't think McTaggart intended or wished or tried to silence anybody; if your question was a silly one, you were shown that it was, without delay; but I

[1] See Dr Broad's Introduction to the 1930 edition of *Some Dogmas of Religion*, p. 46 (Edward Arnold & Co.).

think every pupil always knew and felt that McTaggart was waiting and anxious to hear your justification of your question if you had one, and that it was up to you to produce it. Every utterance must be self-justifying: you were made to concentrate on the inner validity of the thing said, and to feel that this was not the time or place for introspection or for considering how you came to say it. And this I think had on most people a wholesome and stimulating effect. Perhaps for very dull pupils the method was a little crushing, but I should say that no one ever felt there was the smallest degree of unkindness or desire to score on McTaggart's part; and then what can you do with dull pupils in philosophy?

Although now and again, I think I may truly say, I felt really close and very enjoyable contact with McTaggart when I was an undergraduate, I remember that once, a year or two after I went down, I met him in the Great Court, stopped, and began to chat, and he took not the slightest interest in me or any form of gossip that I brought up. The meeting had to be over as soon as possible. On the other hand, when a colleague and I were preparing a translation of Hegel's *Logic* (since published), he gave us, without stint and in the kindest manner, every possible assistance and advice and encouragement."

The impressions given above refer to McTaggart's official lectures, but very shortly after his return from New Zealand in 1899 he announced a popular course for those who knew nothing of philosophy. The object and character of these is indicated in the notice he sent out:

I propose to deliver, in the present academical year, a course of lectures entitled, "An Introduction to the Study of Philosophy". It is chiefly intended for those students who, though not engaged in the systematic study of philosophy, may desire to learn something of the objects, methods, and present problems of metaphysics. No previous knowledge of the subject will be assumed, nor will any course of reading be required in connection with the lectures. The treatment adopted will not be historical, but will deal mainly with the present position of metaphysical enquiries.

No fee will be charged for the lectures, which will be open to all Members of the University, and of Girton and Newnham.

The titles of the lectures were as follows:

Michaelmas Term.
A. Introductory. The relation of Metaphysics to Religion and Science.
B. Scepticism and Agnosticism.
C. Dualism, Absolute and Relative.
D. Materialism and Presentationism.

Lent Term.
E. Dogmatic Idealism.
F. The Critical Position.
G. The Dialectic Position.
H. The Results of Idealism.

Easter Term.
(The subjects of these lectures will be announced later.)[1]

[1] I copy this from the notice of 1902. Possibly the scheme may have been modified in later years, but I doubt it.

I cannot be sure now that I ever attended this course, though I think I must have done so, but I have talked to many people who did and I find general agreement about the stimulating quality of the lectures. McTaggart's wit found special scope here, and his illustrations, taken by preference from the books of Lewis Carroll, and especially from the *Hunting of the Snark*, delighted his audience. The critical part was better understood than the constructive and commanded wider assent. The lectures were continued year after year till the war broke out, and after it was over until the year of McTaggart's death. A very large number of people must have listened to them during those years. Very few of them, no doubt, became philosophers, and perhaps not very many really understood them. But for young men it is very important that they should become acquainted with problems they are never going to solve, have a door opened into a world they will never inhabit and enjoy the scintillations of a brilliant, sincere and imaginative intellect. All these advantages were offered to those who attended McTaggart's course and I do not doubt that many of them profited by them according to the measure of their powers and the quality of their interests. From the educational point of view I suspect that his best work was done there.

This account of McTaggart as a teacher must

not be allowed to crowd out of our minds the more mundane and social aspects of his Cambridge life. He was anything but an ascetic or a prig, as is indicated by the following extracts from letters:

26th May, 1912. To-day is Whitsunday and a Judge, which involves a combination of scarlet and champagne. A feeling of chastened but exquisite happiness comes over me as I think of the approaching evening.

10th January, 1916. We have a Judge in Hall to-night, and I am looking forward to my champagne. I have very youthful tastes for a man of 49. I delight in champagne and in obscenity (if not too healthy) for its own sake, both of which are undergraduate habits. Well, as the sainted Sarah remarked, "Them as is made otherwise, them's different".

This love of conviviality was one of Jack's most obvious characteristics. Dr Broad reports him as saying that "Every undergraduate should be compelled to satisfy his Tutor that he has been drunk at least once a week as a guarantee of good faith that he was not a teetotaller". These *obiter dicta* will not be taken too seriously by those who have a sense of humour. But they are very characteristic. And no doubt McTaggart's love of good fellowship often helped him to form relations with strangers from outside the University.

One of the most notable of these was Sir Francis Younghusband who, in his quest for religious truth, made a pilgrimage to Cambridge to visit the philosopher. It is thus that he describes his interview in his book *The Light of Experience*:[1]

The crucial question I wanted him to help me in settling was whether we were entirely guided and controlled by an outside God, a separate Being altogether from ourselves, or whether we were impelled by an inherent spirit. I had gathered from his books that he held the latter view. In that case I wanted to know whether there was any conscious purpose in that spirit; whether there was any definite end at which it aimed; or whether it was merely a drift or tendency, and, if so, whether we ourselves could direct the tendency and control our destiny. Then I wanted to know what was the goal we should aim at; what was to be our standard of right; what conduced towards our reaching the goal; and whether we had any justification for concluding that good would prevail over evil. Finally, I would ask him where I could find the best metaphysical demonstration of the truth of immortality.

Primed to discuss with him these deepest problems of existence, I called upon him by appointment in his rooms in Trinity College, looking out on to the famous quadrangle. All in the room was scrupulously in order. The furniture was very simple. Rows and rows of books surrounded the room, and each was evidently in its place. And on his desk everything was most neatly arranged. How conducive to study it all was! How different from the scenes in which I had had to pursue my own searchings! I felt a perfect child. Who was I to presume to talk over these profound matters with one who had devoted his whole life to their

[1] P. 213 seq.

study? And if the questions I wanted to ask were formidable, McTaggart himself was no less daunting. He in no way made things easy for me. He was a shy and in many ways an awkward man, and very direct and abrupt. I was afterwards to find that he was full of geniality and humour and agreeable conversation. But no one would call his manner to a comparative stranger winning and ingratiating. I had to make my way through some terrifying defences before I could reach the real man.

My line of approach was through a recitation of my experiences in India. I had been brought very close to Nature in her barest aspects. I had had to deal with people professing all the great religions. Many of these had been deeply interested in philosophical questions. I was interested myself; and now I was home I sought the best advice. Could he help me?

Certainly he would, he replied. So far encouraged, I drew myself together for my main question. It was hard to get it out in this cold-blooded way. But it had to be done. What was his idea of God?

McTaggart now showed himself at his best. He answered directly without any hedging and without any fluffiness of thought.

He explained his general view of the world (which will be exposed in the next chapter) and Sir Francis reports that "my talk with McTaggart had been most valuable to me. Later on", he continues

he asked me to stay with him and took me to dine in hall at Trinity. And here he was a very different man from what he was in his study: he enjoyed a good dinner and a good story as much as anyone. After we had first eaten a big dinner in Hall, and then adjourned to the Common Room for wine, we went on to the well-known Dr Jackson's rooms to smoke and talk. As in the Army so in the University "shop" was eschewed, and there was nothing but good cheer. But walking home I told McTaggart what a privilege I considered it to have his friendship and be able to talk with him upon what had so deeply interested me; and I was surprised at the warmth of feeling with which he replied that the privilege was to him in having the confidence of one who had led such an active life as I had. Evidently McTaggart had an exceedingly sensitive and kind heart as well as a clear head.

The various aspects of McTaggart's character are well illustrated in this account. I will add another record written by one of his many women friends:

Looking back at the golden hours spent in Jack's company, and searching for the secret of his influence an image comes to me, and the more I regard it the more satisfying it is. In *Water Babies* little Tom comes at last to a figure who, while sitting and quietly gazing out over the sea, is yet all the time making creatures make themselves. Well, that's what Jack did.

Little seeds of thought and little sparks of humour burst in his welcoming presence into flowers or flames. I always delighted to save up problems in philosophy or queer questions of ethics for him and when I put them before him his gifts in return were two. The first of course was the joy of seeing a master mind at work, of seeing his marvellous power of picking out the essentials, and grasping the real implications of the problem. But the other, and even more exciting one, was to find that with him one's own mind was twice as acute as before. He indeed made us make ourselves. And it was just the same with humour. Like Falstaff he was not only witty but was the cause of wit in others.

Some of the best hours I have known were spent before that hospitable hearth. A huge fire at one end of the long primrose-coloured room; four chairs; Jack going courteously round with ash-trays and supplies of smokes before we really got down to the talk; the same arrangement usually, with Jack between my husband and me and Daisy on my husband's right. And then, when quite comfortable and smokes going— the talk wouldn't start! The unaccountable shyness that sometimes envelopes friends re-united after months of absence descended, and there we were, tongue-tied. But Daisy would take the situation in hand, and very soon we were all four wanting to talk at once, and when we parted hours later it seemed as if we had hardly begun.

What did we talk about? Well, ourselves, cats, Alice-in-Wonderland, immortality, the newest stories from Trinity high table with chuckles over some of the old chestnuts we loved, God, novels, neighbours, plans for meeting in the holidays, vestments, dreams, ourselves....

The last time Jack stayed in Winchester with us was in March 1913, and I remember vividly a walk we took, just he and I. His talk was fascinating, but I can't recall it, though three piquant little incidents remain. Delighting in his habit of greeting every cat he passed by a salutation, I wickedly started the walk by leading him through a network of back streets in the old town which I knew to be infested with cats. Sure enough, he gave every one a faint acknowledgment with his right hand, as a master passing down College Street would have acknowledged the boys' salutes. We didn't mention cats. Later on our walk led us over grassy downs where the larks were shouting that March morning. I remarked "Aren't the larks glorious?" "Larks, larks!" he exclaimed, peering about on the ground as if I had warned him against rabbit holes, or said the thyme was out! But his enchanting vagueness and absence of mind reached a climax as we returned down a country road. We passed the most striking-looking man I have seen in Europe. Immensely tall, erect, with flashing black eyes but snowy hair, thin as a death mask, in rags of theatrical raggedness, and striding along at a great rate, he was a figure after whom people would naturally turn to gaze. Directly he had passed I asked Jack what he made of him. "I never saw anyone" he said.

I must put on record one kindness of his which touched me specially. His friends know how frightening Jack found children, strange children at any rate. Once when I was ill my two little boys went to stay in Cambridge without me. Jack went and fetched the youngsters, took them down to Trinity to tea in his rooms, showed them all sorts of fascinating things and gave them a great time. A more exhausting effort than delivering a lecture to a distinguished audience.

Apropos of cats in this account, I cannot resist quoting the following from Miss Stawell:

I was laughing at him for the way he spoilt Pushkin: "Why," I said, "I believe if there was only one cosy chair in the room you would give it to Pushkin and take the floor yourself". "Of course I would," he said, "it would be only fair. I could think about the Absolute and I don't believe Pushkin can."

The reminiscences I have cited are by people of Jack's own social class. But he was not, as many of us are, limited in his sympathies to these. He could make friends with anyone if he felt the essential bond of sympathy. For instance, he met once in a train a boy of ten, the son of a charwoman, who had got into trouble with the Director of an open-air camp and been sent away in disgrace. McTaggart fell into conversation with him, learned the facts, and cheered the boy up. And he did not leave the matter there. He kept in touch with the lad, had him down on visits to Cambridge, gave him dinners in town, called upon his mother, and remained his friend till the end. By that time the boy was a youth of seventeen, and two of the most touching letters received by Mrs McTaggart after Jack's death were from him and his mother. Another and rather amusing case is the following. A girl of hysterical tendency had committed a theft and the authorities were inclined to take a serious view of the matter. Mrs McTaggart was indignant. She told Jack about it and Jack, meeting the Mayor the same day, remarked that there was trouble brewing. "But what am I to do?" said the Mayor. "I should do", McTaggart replied, "as the Jesuits used to do when their converts were tiresome, give her a dose of castor-oil." The Mayor departed chuckling, and, though he did not adopt the remedy proposed, handed the case over to Mrs McTaggart to deal with at her discretion.

These are little things to record, but they are useful as giving an idea of McTaggart's vivid and varied personality. Behind all his eccentricities and absentmindednesses, his reserves, his exaggerations of his own paradoxes, his cynical-sounding repudiations of sentimentality, there lay always this warm humanity. The spring of love that bubbled up while he was still a boy at school never ceased to flow, though it may have seemed to be overlaid. Nor did his view of life ever alter throughout the long years of his struggle to demonstrate it by metaphysical reasoning. Of that view something more will be said in a later chapter. Whether or no it is either true or demonstrable, by it and for it Jack lived. His character is not intelligible without it, nor it without his character.

CHAPTER IV

McTAGGART'S FRIENDSHIPS

By PROFESSOR BASIL WILLIAMS

ONE of McTaggart's most notable characteristics was his genius for friendship. Like
most of those who possess this genius, he
probably gave more to his friends than he received: on the other hand he himself received intense happiness from his friendships.

One great source of his capacity for friendship
was his extraordinary sympathy with the thoughts
and lives of men and women very different from
himself: this sympathy gave him a charm of manner
and approach with those in whom he was interested, a charm that with most people soon over-
came the undeniable eccentricities of his ways and
appearance. Moreover he was never handicapped,
as are so many lesser men, by that diffidence that
comes from false modesty or want of purpose and
conviction. This made it easy for him to enter
rapidly into relations with those whose work or
whose outlook on life he admired and to talk with
them naturally on what interested them and him-

self. There was not an element of snobbishness in
his nature, which helped to make him as natural
and devoid of self-consciousness with the simple,
straightforward folk he found on the farms in New
Zealand as with the most eminent in all branches
of life in this country. With men like Arthur
Balfour or Haldane or Thomas Hardy he could
talk at least as an equal in philosophical acuteness
and breadth of vision, and from that basis it was
easy for them and him to talk about their other
interests and activities which were not especially
his own but with which he generally had the
keenest sympathy. At a very early age he had
conceived the most profound admiration for George
Fleming's *Mirage*, and nothing would do for him
but to make her acquaintance. He of course succeeded, and thereafter, almost every time he went
to London, he would give himself the joy of going
to have a talk with her. Men like Sir Francis
Younghusband, as Sir Francis himself recounts on
another page, came to him as enquirers and went
away friends; while on his side McTaggart in one
of his letters tells of his delight at his new friendship with a man whose character and achievements he had long admired from a distance. From
an early stage in his Cambridge career he had
acquired the Cambridge gift of hero-worship of
their great men; and his Cambridge heroes always
were in truth great men, men such as Henry Jack-

son, Marshall, James Ward, the present Master of Trinity, and in later life Lord Rutherford, and perhaps above all that Olympian figure Henry Sidgwick.

Hence it is easy to understand that he was an eminently clubbable man. He especially delighted in dinner talk with those who could exchange appreciations with him of some of his favourite characters in real life or in fiction, such as St Simon, the eighteenth century Duke of Newcastle and any or all of Dickens's personalities. It was something to remember to see and hear him quoting, with breakneck speed and contagious gusto, the utterances of these last, especially, perhaps, Mrs Gamp's or Mrs Wilfer's; indeed, he managed to find in Dickens quotations appropriate to almost every conceivable situation in real life. For example, when he was attending the wedding of a friend and the bride was very late in appearing, he whispered to the lady next to him, "Unalterably, never to be yours, Augusta". At the Savile, a club especially designed to encourage general talk with casual neighbours at lunch or dinner, he was in his element. Not that he was always talking in company. Even with his best friends he sometimes had spells of silence, for he never talked for talking's sake, as some shy or uneasy people do to tide over an awkward pause. With people whom he disliked or with whom he had nothing in common, his silences could become almost devastating. For, though he had a marvellous gift of finding something in common with the most unlikely people, he had a few violent dislikes which nothing could overcome; but even with such he was never consciously rude, for he was essentially the most courteous of men, and if he had a prejudice against a man the worst he did was to try and avoid communication with him. In simple good talk perhaps he was at his best, and that could be brilliant indeed, when he was in company with friends such as the King's trio, Nathaniel Wedd, Roger Fry and Lowes Dickinson, all of them Cambridge contemporaries and one an old school friend. All the four of them knew one another's pet hobbies and weaknesses and would stimulate one another to outrageous statements of their views by running commentaries and extravagantly ribald wit. In such encounters McTaggart generally fought a lone hand, for the others were more liberal and advanced in most of their views, while he to the end maintained the pose of the most obstinate conservatism. But though he generally had the others united against him, he more than held his own by his wealth of apt and stinging quotation and his gift of lightning repartee. There was always good stuff in such talks and they were the most glorious fun.

But with all McTaggart's surface persiflage,

there was never with him any compromise with
actions or views that he thought wrong or harmful.
Men whom he had previously admired and with
whom he had intellectual affinities he broke with
irretrievably because of actions of theirs that he
believed to be incompatible with public duty or
with social rightness. With all his lightness of touch
and his exceedingly broad sympathies, even with
those who differed from him *toto caelo* on politics
or social questions, he had the deepest convictions
about right and wrong both in public and in
personal morality; and any transgression of that
code was to him almost unpardonable.

Allusion has been made to the absence of any
false modesty in him. Indeed he was so confident
in himself because of the work that he felt himself
called upon to do in the world, that he was quite
impervious to ridicule, even of his physical pecu-
liarities or his occasionally odd and unconventional
ways. But of real modesty, the modesty of the
man who knows his aim and believes in it so much
that he is conscious of not having attained it—that
form of modesty he had in abundance. Writing as
a young man to another young man who had not
yet found his object in life, as had some of his
friends, he says:

You must not get discouraged, old man. Of course
you don't happen to have had my good luck and
——'s, in being bitten with a subject which left you

no choice but to follow it out. But lots of men haven't.
...You haven't my conceit, and you haven't had the
advantage of having had your work marked out for
you by other people, as I have a good deal, so that I
had only to work on blindly.

There was not indeed much marking out by others
of his work, nor much blindness in his pursuit of
it; still less was there conceit, unless intense conviction of the value of a life-work undertaken can
be called conceit.

It was just this self-confidence, together with his
unblushing optimism about the world, himself and
his friends, which explains more than anything else
his attractiveness to those very different from himself. It is an interesting commentary on this ex-
uberant optimism of his that only once, perhaps,
in his life he confessed to being glad at getting
away from Cambridge, "and that", he writes,
"was a term when everyone had been ill, and I
had to find the entire stock of my optimism con-
sumed by my acquaintances, which is rather trying". Nor was this optimism a vague, unreasoning
feeling: it was profoundly based on his philosophic
creed, a creed which had far more influence in
moulding his thoughts and his whole attitude to
life than has the religion of most men. A Cambridge friend relates that the last time he saw
McTaggart before his last journey to London was
at a meeting of the Eranos. Throughout the discus-

sion McTaggart had been silent and looked almost uninterested, hunched up as he was in a characteristic attitude with his toes turned in and his head sunk down on his chest. But he had been marking all that was said and at the end came up to this friend and said: "The longer I live, the more I am convinced of the reality of three things: —truth, love and immortality".

To this philosophic creed may also be largely attributed the nature of his deepest friendships, unless perhaps it would be truer to say that his philosophic beliefs were largely based on his conception and experience of such friendships.

To most men he was chiefly known as a philosopher, as a teacher, as a man with a peculiar loyalty to his university, in its most trivial details and ceremonies no less than because of the great objects for which it stands. To a few fortunate men and women, scattered about in the world, he was chiefly known as the most loving, the most faithful and the most tolerant of friends.

Tolerant is perhaps hardly the word; for there was not a trace of condescension in his feelings; charity in the Biblical sense is more expressive of his attitude. For not the least part of his creed was his belief in a possible communion between individuals, each from an understanding of the other's essential nature, a communion that could transcend individual actions and fix itself only on the

personality, of which actions are often merely dim
and delusive representations. His idea of heaven,
or rather of the ultimate destiny of mankind, was
a state in which such understanding would have
developed into a complete comprehension of others,
so that there would be no ignorance, no misunder-
standings, but a knowledge so great as to merge
into all-embracing charity. It was part of his belief
that even in our present stage the glimmerings of
such complete understanding are possible in certain
cases, as he explained in his early pamphlet on
The Further Determination of the Absolute, and more
amply in the second (posthumous) volume of *The
Nature of Existence*.

He had several friends whom he felt he knew
in this almost transcendental way, a knowledge
which, in his belief, came from a complete and
loving understanding of their natures. Most of
these friendships dated from early years and once
made were permanent, being subject to no chances
or changes of circumstance. Distance made no
difference, nor prolonged absence, nor even an
inability of some of such friends quite to understand his point of view. Such friends were of the
most diversified nature: some rather conventional,
others the reverse; some just pleasant unintel-
lectual people, with whom one would think that
he had little—mentally at least—in common; some
capable and successful men of affairs, sure of them-

selves and with a genius for getting on in the world; others again diffident of themselves and tiresome, one might imagine, for the black view they took of the universe. Few of them, perhaps, had his special intellectual gifts and interests; his sympathy found in them, maybe, what he had not got himself and points in which he could give them most. Possibly even those with whom he talked best and with whom he had most in common intellectually were not those of this special band of his most chosen friends.

In two respects McTaggart was specially fortunate and a cause of good fortune to his friends. In the first place, whenever his friends married he almost invariably won the friendship, often the affection, of the new wife or husband; and with him perhaps in no case, as sometimes happens, was the old friendship broken by the change. But fortunate above all for others was McTaggart's own supremely happy marriage. His wife from the first welcomed and made friends of those he had previously cared for. Thereafter his home became in a double sense, and more than ever, one where an understanding and affectionate welcome was assured to his friends.

With regard to his very strong views on certain questions of public and private morality, he was once asked what he would do if one of these special friends committed some disgraceful action: would it make any difference to his affection? Well, he said in effect, in the first place I feel I know the real men or women among these so well, that I am certain that the case would never arise: but, even suppose it did, I do not believe it would make any real difference to my feeling for them, beyond causing me intense grief for the friend and for the pain such action would bring upon him.

Few perhaps of these friends quite realized what he meant to them, when he was among them, seeing them from time to time or, if he could not see them, writing to them throughout his life regularly, once a week perhaps, or at least once a fortnight. Some of these letters, especially in the early days, when he and the rest abounded in the zest of new ideas, were full of good talk about his own and his correspondent's interests. Later, when fundamentals seemed more settled, the letters had perhaps more trivial talk and persiflage, of which he was a master. But at all times they gave the assurance that he was there, immutable and to be relied upon. It mattered not to him whether for long periods his letters were not answered, he was never hurt; he always trusted his friends and would say to himself that they had more important work than he had and were too busy to be able to write. To such friends he was a sure stand-by in a changing world, which is perhaps what he most wished to be, and accorded well with his philosophy. Now

he is dead the memory of that brave and loving
heart is hardly less of an encouragement. As it was
well said by one who knew him not, but knew
something of him and of the quality of his friendship, this special trait in him recalled a saying of
Duns Scotus: "Friendship—the utmost giving of
oneself to another up to the utmost limit of his
power of receiving—is the most perfect moral virtue and the most perfect justice".

CHAPTER V

McTAGGART'S PHILOSOPHY

As we have pointed out more than once, the origin of McTaggart's philosophy was not in his intellect but in his emotions. Unless he had loved he could not have thought as he did. But the love he experienced was transfigured into a finer essence by his imagination and his thought. It is best described in the following passage from an early essay privately printed and not yet published in full, which bears the unpromising title *The Further Determination of the Absolute*.[1]

After describing there in general terms the kind of life which, as he argues, must represent the fundamental nature of spirit, he continues:

What is the concrete and material content of such a life as this? What does it come to? I believe it means one thing, and one thing only—love. When I have explained that I do not mean benevolence, even in its most impassioned form, not even the feeling of

[1] This essay was thought over and, I think, written during his first visit to New Zealand. My copy bears an inscription by the author dated August 1893. Parts of this essay are reprinted in the chapter bearing the same title in his *Studies in Hegelian Cosmology*.

St Francis, I shall have cut off the one probable
explanation of my meaning. When I add that I do
not mean the love of Truth, or Virtue, or Beauty, or
any other word that can be found in the dictionary,
I shall have made confusion worse confounded. When
I continue by saying that I mean passionate, all-
absorbing, all-consuming love, I shall have become
scandalous. And when I wind up by saying that I
do not mean sexual desire, I shall be condemned as
hopelessly morbid—the sin against the Holy Ghost of
Ascalon.

It was, however, some years after his experience
at Clifton before his intellect would allow him to
interpret the universe in terms of his emotions.
When first he went to Cambridge, he was, as we
have noticed, a materialist. But materialism did
not satisfy him. Some way or other, I suppose, he
was bound to find a way out, and he found it in
Hegel. Whether his interpretation of Hegel is correct I am not competent to say. Dr Broad thinks
definitely that it was not.[1] But from that time on
McTaggart's intellectual life consisted in the attempt to work out a dialectic of pure thought
which should establish incontrovertibly his own
idealistic position. In doing so he seems to have
modified seriously and profoundly the actual dialectic of Hegel. But that is a matter for discussion
by specialists. I shall confine myself here to the

[1] See his introduction to the 1930 edition of *Some Dogmas of
Religion*, p. xxxi.

attempt to indicate, for those who are not professional philosophers, what I believe to be the
essence of McTaggart's position.

The essential point was the distinction between
"Reality" and "Appearance". The two were, of
course, in some way connected and part of McTaggart's philosophic aim was to show how. But
nothing could be more unlike "Reality" than the
world of our experience as it appears to us all.
Only in one point was there anything in common
between them. By love, we touch Reality; but only
imperfectly. For we are, or appear to be, imperfect ourselves. We are enclosed in bodies which
perish at death, and it is at best with but a few
of the souls thus fragmentarily revealed that we
come into real contact; whereas in Reality there is
a perfect harmony of all souls, and nothing except
souls is real. Chairs and tables, dishes and plates,
everything that the senses perceive are "really"
souls presenting themselves to our deceptive senses
under these peculiar forms. Something of the kind
seems to have been also Hegel's view. But, by what
seems to be an inconsistency, Hegel was interested
in the actual facts and processes of the world of
"appearance". He wrote, of course, his "pure"
dialectic, but he wrote also a number of what one
might call "applied" dialectics, in which he en-
deavoured to show the "Idea" working itself out
in science, history, art and religion. To the weaker

brethren, such as myself, these applications are the most interesting part of Hegel. But McTaggart set them sternly aside. He saw their logical weaknesses and rejected them in block.

"I am struggling", he says in a letter to a friend, "with Hegel's philosophy of Nature, and what rot it is!" Philosophy must eliminate entirely all considerations of appearance. It must proceed by pure thought. The whole of science was thus cut out at a stroke. McTaggart could be, and was, interested in the men who were pursuing it, for that was part of their work as souls. But he had no belief at all that it threw, or could throw, any light on the real nature of the world.

On the other hand (which might seem self-contradictory) he believed that the world of appearance was moving, on the whole, towards the world of Reality,[1] and that all souls would in the end arrive there. It was a very long, and might be a very terrible, journey. Souls would pass through innumerable incarnations and the most varied destinies before they arrived; and McTaggart himself anticipated very bad times for himself. He would say, as he observed the inhabitants of a slum, that he himself might be thus in some other life; and at times he would console himself for the

---

[1] The possibility of this conception is discussed in a paper called the "Relation of Time to Eternity", printed by the University Press, Berkeley, California, in 1908.

fact that, while he was so happy, his friends were not, by the reflection that his turn for a bad time might come later. There was, however, in all this, one consolation. Friends, he thought, would tend, in the nature of things, to meet again in successive lives. They would not indeed be aware that they had met before, for since we do not remember such meetings now, though they must have occurred in previous incarnations, there is no reason to think we shall remember them in the future. But past intimacies will cause friends to draw together again. "Love at first sight" is to be thus explained —it indicates a previous love in a previous life.

It follows from this general theory that death is not so great a change as is commonly supposed, for the approach to perfection is very slow and gradual. Referring in a letter to the death of a friend he says (Nov. 22nd, 1892):

I doubt if, even now, he knows much more than you or I do. I don't think that death will make so much difference. I should rather imagine that we start from where we left off here and that we learn things very gradually indeed. I have an idea that we are born and die many times and that it is in this way we get on, gaining a little each time.

There have been many idealistic systems of philosophy and some of them as paradoxical as McTaggart's; but in one point, so far as I know, he is unique. He believed in immortality but he did not believe in God. One might indeed say that he had a positive dislike for the conception of God, derived, perhaps, from his earliest family associations. I will cite here a brief passage from a letter which shows his familiar and humorous way of dealing with such questions in the privacy of correspondence:

You are quite wrong about myself and G.A., I mean most decidedly to outlive him. For my own part I propose to be immortal and if he is, I will believe in Herbert Spencer or in any other impossibility you like. Let me refer you to a poem by Mr Algernon Charles Swinburne in *Songs before Sunrise* entitled "Hertha".

Less humorously but in the same strain he writes in December 1898:

You say that Christians have the best of it. Well, they have the belief in heaven and not many other people have it and that is a good thing. (I know very few people who believe as vividly in heaven as I do, but then I am exceptionally lucky.) But it can't be nice to believe in God I should think. It would be horrible to think that there was anyone who was closer to one than one's friends. I want to feel, and I do feel, that my love for them and the same love that other people have for their friends is the only real thing in the world. I have no room left in my life for God, or rather my life is full of God already. I should say, as the Mahometan girl did in Kipling's story, "I bear witness that there is no God save thee, my beloved".

He goes on to express what, so far as I know, was his constant opinion:

Besides, if one was a Christian one would have to worship Christ and I don't like him much. If you take what he said in the first three gospels (for St John's has no historical value I believe) it is a horribly one-sided and imperfect ideal. Would you like a man or a girl who really imitated Christ? I think most of the people I know are living far finer lives than anything you could get out of the gospels. The best thing about him was his pluck at the Crucifixion, and other people have shown as much.

It is with this general scheme of the nature of the world in his mind that McTaggart addressed himself to the concrete problems of human life. Some letters have been preserved which illustrate the curious way in which his mind proceeded in such matters. Here, for instance, is one written on May 18th, 1892, from New Zealand, dealing with the question of pain:

I think that one cannot consider that pain is metaphysically the opposite of pleasure, although no doubt it is so psychologically. But looking at it metaphysically, we must say that pleasure comes from complete self realisation, i.e. complete perfection. But from the greatest possible imperfection would come not complete pain, but rather absence of all feeling. A completely imperfect thing would (on the supposition that the universe is rational) be unable to exist. Pain consequently must be regarded as obeying a formula which makes it equal to zero at each end of the process of the universe, but a real quantity in between. Now pain increases with the development of our sensibilities and aspirations, and diminishes as the universe becomes more capable of satisfying them. And, for the universe as a whole, these two series are the same, for the perfection of the universe would make us more sensitive and also make the universe more satisfactory. Hence pain depends, both directly and inversely, on both the perfection and the imperfection of the universe. Now I think we shall express the facts if we regard the intensity of the pain as the product of the intensities of the perfection and imperfection of the universe.

Let x = amount of pain in the universe at a given time,
z = greatest possible perfection,
y = degree of perfection of the universe at the time in question.

Then $z - y$ = degree of imperfection at that time and our formula will be $x = y (z - y)$. This fulfils the conditions, for $x = 0$ when $y = z$ (i.e. in heaven) or when $y = 0$ (i.e. at the beginning of the process). If this is the formula it follows that the pain in the universe will increase till it reaches the middle of the development (whatever that may be) and then diminish again.

In another letter to the same correspondent, dated September 15th, 1892, he deals with sin:

Prepare yourself to be bored. I have invented a new theory of sin (if this goes on I shall be morbid enough to live in Fitzroy Street) and I want you to hear it. What has always bothered me a good deal, in trying to fit sin into the Hegelian dialectic, was that there seemed to be four terms—original innocence, crime, punishment and repentance. It has now flashed on me that there is one triad with another inside it. We start from innocence and have the process of crime as an antithesis, with virtue as a synthesis. And the crime process is sub-divided into crime itself as a thesis, punishment as an antithesis, and repentance as a synthesis. Putting this into English—we start with the ignorant innocence of paradise which, as Hegel says, is really lower than crime. Here the agreement of your particular conduct with the universal law is merely an accident for you have not known and rejected sin. Accidental conformity with the moral law is, from the point of view of that law, as good as none. This want of real agreement leads you over to sin, which is the want of agreement become explicit. Here you deny the moral law for the sake of your individual will and clearly thereby for the first time the moral law becomes plainly visible. But the only end of will is to seek out good. And we are essentially rational and therefore moral. Our true good must therefore be essentially (inter alia) moral good. Hence to will what is against the moral law is self-contradictory (this, if I am not mistaken, is the position of Socrates). Thus all crime must in the long run bring punishment, for in the long run, given immortality, we must find that our true good is incompatible with crime. Thus punishment asserts a supremacy of the law, as sin does of the individual will. Here we have a contradiction which is solved when the punishment attains its end and reconciles our will to the law. Repentance is thus the synthesis of the subordinate sin process and when it becomes "mittelbar"—that is, is regarded as a

datum for the future, not as a result from the past—
repentance becomes virtue, and thus we gain the
synthesis of sin and innocence. This process can be
repeated indefinitely. For virtue, which is a synthesis
of the main triad, might again become "immediate"
as innocence once more, only innocence on a higher
level. I suppose the reward of virtue gained in one
life is always just the being able to start fresh as a
superior kind of baby when one is born (cf. Rabbi
Ben Ezra, "Fearless and Unperplexed"), and so you
might go on from innocence through crime, punishment, repentance, virtue, to innocence again, until you
had got as high as morality can carry you.

The passages here cited show the style and
character of all his philosophic work. He was aim-
ing at demonstration and he refused to make appeal to anything but reason. But in this attempt
to demonstrate his position he naturally met with
many difficulties and had his periods of depression
and doubt. Sir Francis Younghusband reports
him as saying that, though he believed in immortality and was working out the proof of it by
metaphysics, he had not so far succeeded. He had
found the criticism of the dialectic method by
Bertrand Russell and George Moore very hard
nuts to crack. But he faced the problem with his
usual determination and candour, and it may be
added here that never did he allow a philosophic
dispute to influence his affection and admiration
for his opponents. In the end, I believe, he was

satisfied by the demonstration given in his latest
and posthumous book. But in any case I do not
think that the difficulty of demonstration ever affected his own certainty about the nature of the
world. He had, moreover, to satisfy himself, certain experiences of a mystical kind. He described
them, when they came upon him, as the *Saul*
feeling, and I have already cited above a passage
from his diary noting how that mood came over
him in New Zealand. In using the phrase "the
Saul feeling" he is referring to what was once the
well-known poem of Browning, and as that poet
appears now to be very little read by the younger
generation the passage may be worth citing. The
poem describes how David was summoned to cure
Saul by harping. He tries theme after theme, and
gradually Saul recovers, but one further appeal is
yet needed, and David prophetically strikes the
note of Christ and immortality. He then returns
alone through the night, and his experience is thus
described:

I know not too well how I found my way home in the
    night.
There were witnesses, cohorts about me, to left and
    to right,
Angels, powers, the unuttered, unseen, the alive, the
    unaware:
I repressed, I got through them as hardly, as strug-
    glingly there,

As a runner beset by the populace famished for news—
Life or death. The whole earth was awakened, hell
    loosed with her crews;
And the stars of night beat with emotion, and tingled
    and shot
Out in fire the strong pain of pent knowledge: but I
    fainted not,
For the Hand still impelled me at once and supported,
    suppressed
All the tumult, and quenched it with quiet, and holy
    behest,
Till the rapture was shut in itself, and the earth sank
    to rest.
Anon at the dawn, all that trouble had withered from
    earth—
Not so much, but I saw it die out in the day's tender
    birth;
In the gathered intensity brought to the grey of the
    hills;
In the shuddering forests' held breath; in the sudden
    wind-thrills;
In the startled wild beasts that bore off, and each with
    eye sidling still
Though averted with wonder and dread; in the birds
    stiff and chill
That rose heavily as I approached them, made stupid
    with awe:
E'en the serpent that slid away silent—he felt the
    new law.
The same stared in the white humid faces upturned
    by the flowers;
The same worked in the heart of the cedar and moved
    the vine-bowers:

And the little brooks witnessing murmured, persistent
    and low,
With their obstinate, all but hushed voices—"E'en so,
    is it so!"

It is evident that to McTaggart this "Saul feeling" was something very real. But it is not easy,
nor perhaps possible, to know precisely what it
was. Mrs McTaggart tells me of an occasion when
he had been at a College meeting which had tired
and worried him. He walked home by the Backs.
It was a cold winter day, and there was snow on
the trees and the ground, but on his return Jack
told her that suddenly the whole scene had changed.
The trees had budded, the birds had burst into
song, and, as she insists, this was not merely a
piece of imagination but an actual perception of
the senses. Jack never spoke, so far as I know, to
of these experiences any of his friends. But there
is one interesting reference in a letter he wrote to
Sir Francis Younghusband. He is referring to an
experience Sir Francis had had in the mountains
of Thibet on the day he left Lhasa, and which he
thus describes in his book, *The Heart of Nature*
(p. 168):

I had a curious sense of being literally in love with
the world. There is no other way in which I can express
what I then felt. I felt as if I could hardly contain
myself for the love which was bursting within me. It
seemed as if the world itself were nothing but love.

We have all felt on some great occasion an ardent glow of patriotism. This was patriotism extended to the whole Universe. The country for which I was feeling this overwhelming intensity of love was the entire Universe. At the back and foundation of things I was certain was love—and not merely placid benevolence but active, fervent, devoted love and nothing less. The whole world seemed in a blaze of love, and men's hearts were burning to be in touch with one another.

Referring to this passage McTaggart writes:

It is a great help and comfort to know that people feel the same as oneself, especially to find that a man whose outward life has been so different from mine as yours has been has found his way to the same inner reality. My experience has been like what you describe—on one occasion, especially, in one of the great churches at Rouen, and once in the National Gallery. I think the best description I know of it are the last lines of Browning's "Saul"—those that begin

"I know not too well how I found my way home in the dark".

Sir Francis continues:

McTaggart then proceeded to pronounce a judgment on this experience with which I agreed at the time but with which I definitely disagree now. He said, "It is, I think, the highest thing in life but one. Love—just the love of one person for another—is the highest of all. If they could be united at the same moment, if the love for one person could be felt as what did sum up the whole Universe, that would be

the culmination of all things. But that I have not
felt yet, though I believe it to be true".[1]

It is clear, from this statement, that McTaggart
felt his own experience to be of the same kind as
that of Sir Francis, and that it involved a direct
perception that Love is the essence of Reality. The
experience no doubt was evidence to him of the
truth of his philosophy; but he never allowed
himself to put it forward as evidence, because
he believed that he was called and was able to
demonstrate the truth by pure reason.

On the other hand he disagreed with Sir Francis
in one important point. He believed, as we have
seen, in the harmony of immortal spirits, but not
in any higher Spirit that included them. Referring
to this point, he says in a letter to Sir Francis:

I should agree that God (if you think best to call
it God) stands to the selves as the regiment does to
the soldiers. But I should not call either God or the
regiment a personality. And I should not hold that
God has any intrinsic value—the only intrinsic value
is in the selves, though they only have it because they
are united in the Divine Unity.

As to the nature of that union, he says in another
letter:

I conceive the self as like a jet of water. All the
more so because fountains spread out as they reach
the top. I think of us as a fountain the culmination

---

[1] *The Light of Experience*, pp. 217–218.

of whose efforts is to reach the heights at which they will directly touch one another.

There is nothing in McTaggart's printed works about this experience. But there is an interesting paper on Mysticism in the *New Quarterly*, July 1909. He there argues that mysticism in the proper sense implies two elements—"firstly, a mystic unity, and secondly a mystic intuition of that unity", and of these he says that the former is the more fundamental. The discussion proceeds in his usual manner by distinctions and definitions. McTaggart does not say definitely that he himself had had mystic experiences, but a passage towards the end is very significant for his biography. He raises the question whether a man is justified in contemplating one side of Reality, the unity, and ignoring the other, differentiation, because the former gives him happiness and the latter does not, and he concludes as follows:

I can see no reason why a man should not act in this way. And if happiness is good there is a very obvious reason why he should act in this way since it would increase his happiness. In the ordinary affairs of life action on such a principle would be generally approved. Suppose that the view from the eastern windows of my house is beautiful while the view from the western windows is ugly. I shall act very absurdly if I assert that I have no western windows or if I assert that the view is beautiful. And I shall act wrongly if I refuse to look out from them when there is any practical advantage in doing so—if, for example, I could form and carry out a scheme for improving the prospect. But when I have recognized the ugliness, and if I cannot improve it, shall I be doing wrong if I look by preference eastward to beauty? Should I not rather be doing wrong if I acted in any other way? In like manner the mystic whom we are now considering, turns his attention from that which he judges to be evil, or which he temporarily finds distasteful, to that which gives him happiness. He will be less fortunate than that other mystic who finds all reality good—the differentiation as well as the unity. But he will act rightly for he will gain happiness—and happiness is good. And if happiness differs in quality it is of no ignoble kind.

What I have been saying here of McTaggart's philosophy is only what a layman can gather who once knew him well and in early youth read much philosophy with him. A more authoritative exposition of his position by Mr S. V. Keeling, Senior Lecturer of University College, London, will be found in chapter VIII.

CHAPTER VI

GENERAL READING AND
POLITICAL OPINIONS

LIKE many men who lead a strenuous intellectual life, Jack had a passion for novels. At an early age he read through the whole collection of the Union library. His method was to write down the names of the books in a notebook and then to read them in such an order that, as he scratched off those he had read, he made a certain pattern on the page. He would start with the one on the top of the page, go on to the one at the bottom, then to the top but one and the bottom but one, and so on, until the scratchings off met in the middle. He would read at least a novel a day, sometimes several, by preference while he lay in his hot bath. Yet he never seemed to forget any of them. And though he was thus omnivorous he was not really indiscriminate in his taste. He knew pretty well what was good literature and what was not, though his taste could be easily diverted if something appealed strongly to his sentiment. He had a passion for Dickens, which I shared, and on our expeditions on the river he was continually reading and citing him. In earlier days he and his sister Susan used to rehearse whole scenes between Mrs Wilfer and Lavvy, and in later life after his marriage he would shut himself up with his wife on Saturday evenings and enact with her assistance long passages from Pickwick. He was also one of the many who were intrigued by the problem of Edwin Drood, and I find in one of his letters a long dissertation on this subject. He also admired both Hardy and Meredith. Of the former he made the personal acquaintance and Hardy wrote him two letters which are worth citing here:

23rd May, 1906.

DEAR SIR,

Quite by chance I took up from the table here a day or two ago your recent work *Some Dogmas of Religion* (to which I was attracted by seeing on its back a name I have been familiar with in the pages of *Mind*, etc.) and I think I ought to write and tell you what a very great pleasure the reading of the book has given me, though this is a thing I very seldom do. The clearness, acuteness and vigour of the thinking throughout, its entire freedom from sophisms and the indubitable moral good to be derived from a perusal of it are cheering to others whose minds have run more or less in the same groove but have rather despaired of seeing harmful conventions shaken—in this country at least—by lucid argument and, what is more, human emotions.

My own personal connection with the subject is

merely that in a book of which I have published a
portion, *The Dynasts*, I have vaguely sketched a philosophic basis for the drama, or poem, or whatever it
may be called, which is not far from what you suggest
by your negative conclusions.

With many thanks for the book,

I am,

Yours truly,

THOMAS HARDY.

22nd August, 1908.

DEAR MR McTAGGART,

I am reading *The Relations of Time and Eternity*[1] with
much more interest than I expected from the title
(many thanks for the copy). I go quite with you in
your argument. Sections 23, 24, 25, in which you
grapple with ordinary experiences, are illuminating.
26 and 27 are as much as ever can be said for possi-
bilities, I think. However I am not a trained philosopher as you are (though I do read *Mind* occasionally).
As a mere empiricist I have the common-place feeling
that the Timeless Reality knows no difference between
what we call good and what we call evil, which are
only apparent to the consciousness of organic nature
generally—which consciousness is a sort of unantici-
pated accident: so that no dignified philosophy can
be built up out of the unworthy materials at our com-
mand.

Yours truly,

THOMAS HARDY.

[1] Printed by the press of the University of California, Berkeley,
1908.

In 1920 he read Lawrence's *Rainbow*, which had been seized by the police, and he remarks: "It isn't exactly Sunday School literature, but it seems to me—as far as I can remember—that the *Kreutzer Sonata* was at least as obscene and very much duller". This judgment may seem to some of us surprising, but it is explained by what follows: "But then of course Tolstoi had a high moral purpose. What we really want is a law against high moral purposes—or at any rate against exposing them in public".

He was attracted by books which were either concerned with the atmosphere of places or contained something mystic in their theme. *Mirage* by George Fleming was a great favourite, read again and again. Flora Annie Steele was also a favourite, particularly *The Potter's Thumb* and *The Prince of Dreams*. He was devoted to Richard Jefferies, particularly *Bevis*. The last novel that he ever read was Galsworthy's *White Monkey*. Of this he greatly approved. Of recent works suggesting more than meets the eye he was particularly intrigued by Garnet's *Lady into Fox* while frankly confessing his inability to understand what the author would be at.

His reading of poetry, as of novels, was omnivorous. His favourite poet appears to have been Swinburne. The anapaests obviously excited his not too critical rhythmical sense. He would read

Swinburne in his bath and turn to him for relief whenever things were going wrong in his universe. He liked especially *Dolores* and he liked all poets who dealt with religious or philosophic themes, such as Clough and Omar Khayyam. Shakespeare he seems to have read with genuine enthusiasm, selecting for this purpose, every year, the Christmas festival. For Pope he had a great admiration:

How magnificent he is at his best! There were people (I daresay there are people) who say he is not a poet. If the first book of the *Essay on Man*, the end of the *Dunciad* and the character of Atticus were not written by a poet, poets must be very remarkable people.

He also admired Crabbe: "The better things are certainly tedious as a whole, but *The Village* and *The Borough* are tremendously good". On which follows the humorous remark:

I am shocked, however, to find a respectable clergyman like Crabbe saying that perhaps hell might not be unending! Walter Scott expresses the same revolting scepticism. I wonder if he got it from Crabbe. He was very fond of him.

For Shelley he never cared. The poet might have appealed to one side of McTaggart's character—his passion for metaphysics and for love. But then Shelley was a republican, and had no respect for British institutions or the British type of character. He was sent down from Oxford and driven out of England. He was in fact a rebel through and through; whereas Jack in just those matters where Shelley was radical became increasingly a Tory. Whichever element in the philosopher may be regarded as the Jekyll or the Hyde, Shelley represented only one of them, and I don't think that McTaggart at all approved of him. He would probably have liked some things of Goethe, but I never heard of him reading them, perhaps because his knowledge of German was not good enough for him to get the flavour of the poetry. He did, however, refer with approval to Goethe's low bow when he met royalty in the street, in contrast to Beethoven, who strode by with his hat crushed over his eyes and made no sign. His determination to read through from beginning to end even the inferior works of any one he read at all enabled him to discover some gems, one of which is so amusing that I insert it here. He has been reading, he says, Young's poem on the Day of Judgment in which he

introduces (for reasons left obscure) Jonah and the whale. The meeting of these historical characters is very beautifully described:

"The whale expands his jaws' enormous size;
  The prophet views the cavern with surprise;
  Measures the monstrous teeth, afar descried,
  And rolls his wond'ring eyes from side to side;
  Then takes possession of the sacred seat
  And sails secure within the dark retreat."

The second line seems to me one of the most perfect in the English language. The third morning "sees the king of waters rise and pour His sacred guest uninjured on the shore".

He goes on:

After these sacred heights I cannot descend to merely secular subjects, and can only bring myself to tell you of the comment on King's Chapel made by a convalescent Canadian. "Well, this is some missionhouse!"

In another letter he refers to James Thomson, whom he is reading on Sundays:

(6th December, 1924.) I have nearly finished that distinguished poet. I have read *Alfred*, in which immortal work we find Rule Britannia—I had quite forgotten he wrote it. Also *Sophonisba*, but the line "Oh Sophonisba, Sophonisba, Oh!" which caused the damnation of the play is left out. Good heavens, he is bad!

In history he had a great delight in memoirs and letters, and his infallible memory enabled him to store an amount of knowledge which not all professed historians attain. He delighted in Walpole's Letters and even trespassed (by an exception, I think) upon the memoirs of La grande Mademoiselle in French. It is amusing to insert the following passage dealing with that book:

(7th *July*, 1923.) I think I told you I was reading the Memoirs of Mademoiselle. I am still engaged in doing so, for her Royal Highness is rather lengthy. I found a nice passage yesterday, about a certain M. de Chaudemier. "Je le trouve devenu philosophe; il croyait le monde tout autrement qu'il n'étoit." This is about as good as Johnson's friend who couldn't be a philosopher because cheerfulness was always breaking in. As a rule H.R.H. is not very amusing, but on one occasion, when she wished to be formally incognito on a journey, and people insisted on coming to her with addresses, she remarked out of the coach window "je ne suis pas moi", which seems to me to have great depth in it.

Referring to vol. II of Mr Simpson's *Napoleon III*, which he had not yet read, he says:

I hope there will be much about his mistresses (as far as I remember there was a fair amount in the first volume). Mistresses are so much more interesting than visits to Queen Victoria or great exhibitions (the word "his" in the last sentence refers to his late Imperial Majesty and not to the Dean of Chapel).

Literature, however, except where it touched him on the side of philosophy and mysticism, was not of the first importance in his life. On the other hand it sometimes seemed that his political opinions were more to him even than his philosophy; perhaps, as is suggested below, because he had persuaded himself that the principal means to the realization of the kingdom of heaven was the British Empire. It is true that at school, as we have seen, he was an advanced radical, expressing and defending unpopular views with all his habitual courage. But the school had its revenge, for as soon as McTaggart became a recognized institution there his loyalty to the place began to override everything else. Henceforth, broadly speaking, loyalty was the basis of his views—loyalty, first to Clifton and by extension to all public schools, next to Cambridge and by extension to Oxford, next to Great Britain (Ireland, or at least what is now the Free State, he never included in his scheme), next to New Zealand and, by extension, to the other self-governing parts of the Empire. The origin and character of his political opinions is well described in the following letter from Professor Basil Williams:

It is perfectly true, I think, that Jack always took the crudely Jingo views of politics, especially in foreign relations. I think in giving an account of such views it is important to relate them with his views on public schools. In that respect also he was a Tory of the Tories, believing that all that is good in public schools comes from the old-fashioned idea of "spare the rod and spoil the child", with a strong belief in fagging and very strict discipline and the cultivation of all the robuster virtues. In that respect he drew his reasons, I imagine, though I don't think I ever put to him the question, from what must have been his own experience. I cannot believe that a peculiar person such as he was could have escaped a good deal of ridicule and probably also a good deal of bullying in his early days at Clifton, and yet, in the long run, he held his place there and kept his ideas simply by dogged perseverance: and on looking back at his own experiences there came to the conclusion that if you have anything original in you, as he certainly had, you get strengthened rather than weakened by the very drastic discipline that you have to overcome both from the school discipline and from the dislike of schoolboys for anything out of the ordinary. He made good and retained, even sharpened, his own originality by the process, and therefore thought such strenuous discipline good for others. He was a genius of very strong personality that nothing could overcome, and forgot that other geniuses with perhaps slightly weaker personalities might be entirely overwhelmed by such a system. And I correlate his extremely virulent, if I may use the epithet, patriotism with this school theory. He had made up his mind, like Rhodes, at a very early period that the best thing in the world for its advance and gradual approach to God, as Rhodes would have said,—to the ultimate harmony, as I imagine Jack would have said,—was to be found in making British ideas, by force if need be, predominant over the whole world.

This did not mean that he accepted all the current ideas of the Tory creed in internal politics. He was a Liberal in many respects in state affairs quite as much as in university affairs. When few believed in women's suffrage, he was staunch for it, and in general he was all for the most open expression of views that might be heterodox in sex matters, in religious matters and in economic theory. Where he drew the line was in times of national danger, when he thought that what seemed to him the safety of the nation was involved. . . . The fact of the matter with Jack was that, fairly early in his life, he had come to certain definite conclusions about the British Empire, about public schools and certain other matters of great moment to him indeed, but still not directly connected with his life work, and then left them at that as a basis from which he deduced his views on particular details connected with those matters.

Probably also his political views were affected by the character of his philosophy. In the first place, what seems to most people to be the real world he believed to be only apparent, and though he always protested against the idea that evil is not real, yet, after all, it was only transient and in the long run—a very long run, it is true—did not much matter. In the second place, the Dialectic proceeded by contradictions and conflicts, so that conflict assumed not only a necessary but even an admirable character. To cite Mr Wedd:

His Hegelian philosophy taught him that spiritual evolution occurs as the result of conflict between two goods leading on to a higher good, which in its turn develops a contradiction, splits up into two opposing tendencies, the reconcilement of which results in a yet higher good and so on until at some inconceivable point in the distant future the process culminates in a good that develops no contradiction in itself but contains all the reality of all the imperfect manifestations of good that have gone before. This culmination is called the Absolute. That there was such a culmination fixed for all inevitably to attain became, under the teaching of Hegel, McTaggart's settled conviction.

Viewed from this standpoint, social wrongs, injustice, misery of all kinds, are seen to be imperfect manifestations of good, necessary stages in the evolution of a higher good. One convinced of this philosophy may seem to regard wrong with a callous indifference. The true Bolshevist fervour, an adherent of Lenin has rightly noted, can only be realized by one who is convinced that this life is all we have, that the material things are the only values that count, that anything beyond this life, and any values other than the material, are the dope administered by the privileged few to rob the many of their rightful share of the good things of life. If you regard existence as not confined to this one life of seventy years but, as McTaggart came to regard it, as a series of reincarnations during each of which the individual spirit rises higher in the scale of being until it and all other individuals reach perfection and are united each to all the others in a relationship of perfect love, then the struggle to grasp the material pleasures of an ephemeral existence is seen to be an imperfect expression of the aim and meaning of life.

While he was a boy at school and a freshman at college, McTaggart held the former of these two conflicting views. He proposed to devote himself to the amelioration of the material conditions of life for the mass of the people. In fact, he proposed to become a politician on radical lines. Somewhere about the beginning of his second year he discovered Hegel and his habitual intrepidity led him to revise all his beliefs in the light of the new truth, and he found as a result of the revision that few of his old political beliefs remained. His desire for the happiness of others remained as strong as ever. His view of what constituted happiness, and still more his view of how happiness was to be attained, underwent a radical change. It is not through the *cloaca maxima* that you reach the city of God, and that city, when reached, is not paved with material gold. His deflection from the beliefs of his childhood seemed to many of his early friends an inexplicable deterioration. One of those friends was Mr M., an artist and a neighbour at Weybridge, a friend of Jack's mother in her early widowhood, who helped her in all business affairs and took the keenest interest in all her children. Mr M. was a man of beautifully simple character, devoted to his art, and desiring happiness for all the downcast and dispossessed. He detested the purse-proud, the snobbish, the indifferent, and he had warmly welcomed the early signs of Jack's radical philanthropy. To him, as to others, it came as a great shock to find that a few years at Cambridge had converted the philanthropist and the radical into an apparently callous Tory, tolerant of all the iniquities of society, and I remember that on the occasion of a visit of the artist to the McTaggart family in their haunt at Embleton on the Northumbrian coast, which M. had discovered for them, a regular family conclave was held at which I was present, to discuss the question of Jack's deflection from the dreams of his youth. I too, at that time, was an ardent radical. Difference of political opinion did not form an obstacle to friendship with McTaggart, but I too felt puzzled by the change in his attitude. Most light was thrown on our debate by the remark of Jack's elder sister, Margaret, that the Esquire Bedells were the real cause of Jack's change of front. By this she meant that the glamour of ancient institutions like those of Cambridge, rooted in a distant past and conveying through the ages the most valuable treasures of the human mind, seemed to make ready-made schemes for the reformation of society, on lines of shallow, if well-intentioned, theories, look preposterous, like a garden city of jerry built cottages and corrugated iron places of worship springing up to confront with their pert appearance and replace with their pretentions of modernity the stately homes and historic cathedral of some ancient city, which have grown in the course of the centuries with the growth of the English spirit. The age and beauty of Cambridge, both in its spiritual and its physical manifestations, made the secularist, machine-made, philanthropic ideals of his boyhood seem unamiable and garish.

While this was the general character of McTaggart's political opinions, it must not be concluded that they were on all points what used to be called conservative. He was, for instance, always a free-trader. We have seen how he lectured in favour of free trade to recalcitrant New Zealanders. He adhered to that position until the end of his life and I do not think he would have changed it now, although, now that free trade is regarded as an out-worn superstition, perhaps his belief on that subject should be added to the corpus of his Tory prejudices. Again, he had always believed in women's suffrage, this because he had always believed in the equality of the sexes, and I should suppose, though I do not know, that he would have welcomed the appearance of women not only on administrative bodies but in Parliament. But apart from these two points, certainly not unimportant ones, Jack was during the greater part of his life a consistent Tory. On the question of the House of Lords I remember him once suggesting that the only reform he would propose would be the addition of all those bishops who do not at present have seats there. About the House of Commons he always assumed a cynical eighteenth-century attitude that corruption was the best way to get a good house. He believed that politicians should be strong party men, quoting Major Pendennis to the effect that "A virtuous attachment is the very deuce". To Irish Home Rule he was always opposed and the following extract from a letter is not merely satirical:

8th September, 1892.

I am reading Duffy's *Four Years of Irish History*. Among other things he says that not one letter in ten of those exchanged among the Irish leaders in '45 and '49 was dated. Does not this explain why Ireland never was and never will be free? It reminds one of Elizabeth's Earl of Essex who, according to Froude, when he wished to be particularly precise used to date his letters "This morning". While the Irish people remain like that I don't think that we shall have much Home Rule at work whatever Gladstone may do.

To any scheme of Church disestablishment he was in his later life opposed, as might be expected when we consider, not his actual religious views, but his delight in the institution. "Every year", he writes, "that we can delay the Church question makes it more probable that we shall save Scotland and the four Welsh dioceses. As for the bulk of the English Church I believe they might as well try to abolish the multiplication table." On this point, however, I think his opinions may have oscillated, for I remember him remarking in earlier life when the proposal for disestablishment without disendowment was in the air that it reminded him of Mr Wegg's famous remark: "With the single exception of the salary I resign the whole sitiwation". What he would have thought in the present situation I do not know, but I suspect that he would have wished to retain the connection with the State.

While McTaggart, as we have seen, held certain views that used to be regarded as Liberal, he never seems to have had any sympathy with the political ideas of Labour. One need not take too seriously an amusing remark attributed to him when he heard that certain trade unionists were critical of a well-known labour leader because he had never done any manual work. "Nothing could be more unjust", McTaggart retorted, "his hands are horny with wire-pulling." But in his later life he was a strong antagonist of the Labour Party. Thus in January 1924 he writes:

The collapse of the triple alliance strike gave me great pleasure. I have no sympathy with the miners as things stand. One can certainly excuse considerable irritation at such large drops in wages, and very possibly they were in some cases too large. But when they stopped the pumping they put themselves so utterly in the wrong that I should not pity them— though for the sake of the country I should regret it—if they were forced by hunger into a complete surrender.

On the other hand, in his personal relations McTaggart always retained that freedom from class prejudices which had been so conspicuous in New Zealand. When he and his wife were staying at Embleton, a little village in Northumberland where they used to go for their summer holiday, he used to attend the village dances and concerts and make easy acquaintance with the people. He also attended meetings both of the miners and of the masters in the then bitter mining crisis, insisting that it was necessary to hear both sides. He was invited at one of these meetings to make a speech himself and rather disgruntled his audience by telling them that if they continued to spend all their money on food and fun for themselves and left their wives without necessary household stuff they would find that before long they would not be able to get wives at all.

From this brief sketch of McTaggart's political attitude it will be seen to be inevitable that when the war broke out he should be wholeheartedly and without any doubts or qualifications on the side of England and her allies, without either desiring or attempting to know anything about the real causes and the probable effects of the catastrophe. Unfitted by physique and age for service at the front, he did all he could to help the war by working in a munitions factory and taking office as a special constable. He used to parade Cambridge, when his turn came, in the small hours of the night, and call up anyone at any house where he saw a glimmer of light. These activities, the only ones of which he was capable, I have no doubt that he carried out in the same spirit in which, under other circumstances, he would have gladly offered his life. Since, as it happened, some of his Cambridge friends took a different view, the tension between him and them became extreme. It came to a head when McTaggart took a leading part in the expulsion of Bertrand Russell from his lectureship. I feel sure, however, that in the action he took McTaggart was free from all personal animosity. He took his stand on the view that Trinity could not condone an actual breach of the law and that Russell had been guilty of that when he published, albeit in a very obscure publication, the words which were the excuse for his arrest. This is not the time or place to enter into that controversy. It need only be remarked that McTaggart's conduct was consistent with his views and principles and that he never, so far as I know, allowed his adherence to what he conceived to be a duty to affect his personal feelings to his friends. In the difficult years after the war he always played the part of a reconciler at Trinity. On the other hand, even when the war was over, his anti-German passion remained intense and unreconciled. "I wish", he writes at the time of the invasion of the Ruhr, "that we hadn't separated from France. Of course our Treasury may be right, and very probably is. But I wish it had been economically possible to take more drastic action against Germany." Again he says in August of the same year:

There is a Liberal Summer School going on in the town and many Liberals find their way to dinner when I excite their abhorrence by remarking, when invited to hate militarism, that I consider that Germany has a claim on the limited amount of hatred I have available (for the matter of that I doubt if there is any chance of militarism in our generation except in Germany and possibly Russia).

It should be added that so far as I know McTaggart had no belief or interest in the League of Nations and believed in nothing but a strong navy for the protection of British interests.

If we turn now from national to university politics, the whole position is altered. McTaggart here is a radical in all important matters. He was, of course, an advocate of women's degrees. He supported the proposal to abolish compulsory Greek for the Little-Go. He writes in December 1902:

You ask me about Greek. I shall vote for the change. I think that the retention of Greek will not keep Greek in the schools since the schoolmasters know that it can be crammed up by the few boys who are going into the universities in a few weeks. So it will drop from the smaller schools whatever we do, and I do not think that whatever we do it will drop from the big schools. Besides I think that a better fight can be made for liberal education as against technical if we don't practically take up the position that there is no liberal education without Greek—a position which is false and which would alienate us from the support of liberal education in the Scotch and provincial universities. The proper attitude, I think, is that though some studies cannot be made liberal (dentistry, for example, and agriculture are such, at least in the present) yet no one study is essential to a liberal education. At Oxford I believe some people would deny this. Here no one would—not because we see further but because our traditions always asserted that mathematics and classics were of equal dignity. But if you can have a liberal education without seriously pursuing classics it seems to be absurd to fight for a mere smattering.

He was also in favour of a government commission to enquire into the working of the University. When the question was being mooted in 1906 he writes:

I shrink with selfish horror from the idea of the loss of time a commission would be, and I should like the initiative to come from the University rather than from the State. But I am so radical academically that I think I should welcome most of the changes such a commission would probably make. I should anticipate: (1) Equality for women; (2) No compulsory Greek; (3) Some condition for the M.A.; (4) Teaching to be more university and less college; (5) Abolition of mere prize fellowships; (6) A poverty test for the money of scholarships; (7) Something done to heads of colleges. All these I should welcome. I do not see what else they would be likely to do. Any revision of stipends, except in a few cases, would mean an increase for I think we are not paid above current rates.

It is interesting to note that the principal of these reforms have actually been carried out since the recent Commission. Of the movement which led to the appointment of that Commission in 1919 he said:

We have had a report from the Council of the Senate requesting us to decide whether we shall apply for government aid, which will involve a Commission. I imagine we shall decide to do it. I am in favour of doing it. As for a Commission we should probably have had one soon whether there was a grant or not and I want a Commission, firstly because, though we have doubtless many faults, I believe we are both more efficient and more economical than most outsiders think and I should like to have that fact brought before the public. Secondly, because there are one or two reforms in the University which I believe a Commission would give us and which for various reasons it is almost impossible to get without a Commission. Nor am I much afraid of government interference. At the same time I should hope that the grants to the universities would continue to be made by a Treasury Committee and not handed over to the Board of Education.

In conclusion, his half-humorous but wholly sincere zeal for university institutions may be illustrated from the following letter of 1910:

What do you think has happened? I must put it in red ink I HAVE CREATED DOCTORS! Aren't you glad you married me? They asked me at the morning congregation to create the Doctors in Letters, but I pointed out (what no one else seemed to realize) that they couldn't be created separately from the Doctors in Science. . . . I came back in the afternoon and found Reid and Lapsley there, so I thought I should not be senior. But they left, and I did it. I created the beautiful doctors. I found to my horror at the last moment that I had to turn the candidates' Christian names and their colleges into Latin. All I can say is that I didn't make as many mistakes as Clifford Albutt did. I wish you had been there to see me put on my bonnet before the Vice-Chancellor! The V.C. had left the chair, and dissolved the congregation, so that the Creators—Swete, Higgins, All-butt, me, and the Deputy Senior Proctor, were the presiding authorities—which takes one back a very long time in the history of the University.

Chapter VII

THE END

McTAGGART's death at the age of fifty-eight was altogether unexpected. Apparently still in the prime of his powers, he visited London with his wife in December 1924. He was attacked by severe pain in the leg, which was at first attributed to sciatica. As it got worse he was removed to a nursing home and diagnosis showed that the pain was due to a clot of blood. There were, indeed, several such and it was impossible to save his life. Two clots actually passed through his heart, but that he survived almost by a miracle. After that the doctors gave him morphia and he died unconscious on January 18th, 1925.

For a man of McTaggart's belief the approach of death was the crowning test. Could he meet it as what he had always affirmed it to be, a mere passage into another life? He passed the test triumphantly. When he was told that he must die he said to his wife: "I am grieved that we must part, but you know I am not afraid of death". The nurses and doctors in attendance were astonished. "What is this man", they asked. "A philosopher?"

"Well, I never knew a philosopher was so serene."
When he recovered from the first heart attack he
joked with his nurse, remarking that it was amusing
that he should be attended at the last by a Roman
Catholic. As he had lived, so he died, unshaken
in his happiness and his faith. The truth of his
philosophy many philosophers would deny, many
men doubt, and most be unable to estimate; but
true or no, his pilgrimage through life was directed
from the beginning to the end by the twin stars
of truth and love. Like all the great philosophers
he not only thought but believed his philosophy;
and whatever may be the fate of his ideas his
memory in the hearts of his friends is secure. He
was their dear, their faithful, their never-changing
Jack.

It was not, however, only his more intimate
friends who felt a singular affection for him. The
letters written to his wife after his death show how
widely and sincerely his loss was felt among the
most various kinds of people. There are letters in
Cambridge from men engaged in every branch of
study, from physicists, lawyers, doctors, theologians,
as well as those engaged in university business.

But these were not all. There is a letter expressing
the regrets of the college servants. There are letters
from the boy he met in the train, and from his
mother. There is another from a working man at
Embleton; another from an Italian waiter in Italy

Wherever he had turned he had made and kept friends; and his best epitaph is the sentence of F. H. Bradley, prefixed to his essay on the *Further Determination of the Absolute*:

To love unsatisfied the world is a mystery,
A mystery which love satisfied seems to comprehend.

McTAGGART'S METAPHYSICS

by

S. V. KEELING

M.A., D.-ès-L., Officier d'Académie,
Senior Lecturer of University College,
University of London

CHAPTER VIII

McTAGGART'S METAPHYSICS

THAT McTaggart was a philosopher of singular originality and penetration and one in whom clear and rigorous reasoning was developed to an exceptional degree is presumably evident to readers of this Memoir. But the eminence to which his work in metaphysics raises him may not have been fully appreciated. Few, indeed, even among professional philosophers, have so far assigned him to what I dare believe is his proper place. It was McTaggart's considered opinion that on the whole Hegel had penetrated further into the truth about reality than any of his predecessors. And it may well happen before our century has grown old that it will estimate McTaggart's life-work in the same terms. Among contemporary philosophers probably none has so detailed and exact a knowledge of McTaggart's own system as Dr C. D. Broad[1], and

[1] Dr Broad, who succeeded McTaggart as Lecturer in the Moral Sciences at Trinity College, Cambridge, has written a brilliant notice on his predecessor, which was published in the *Proceedings of the British Academy* for 1927, and reproduced, with slight modification, as an Introduction to the Second Edition of McTaggart's *Some Dogmas of Religion* in 1930.

he has declared it a work of genius which places its author "in the front rank of the great historical philosophers", and one that "may quite fairly be compared with the *Enneads* of Plotinus, the *Ethics* of Spinoza, and the *Encyclopaedia* of Hegel". This "complete system of *a priori* metaphysics on the grand scale" occupies, in Dr Broad's opinion, "a unique position in English philosophical literature". He goes on to add:

> The system expounded in the *Nature of Existence* is equal in scope and originality to any of the great historical systems of European philosophy, whilst in clearness of statement and cogency of argument, it far surpasses them all. If subtle analysis, rigid reasoning and constructive fertility, applied with tireless patience to the hardest and deepest problems of metaphysics, and expressed in language which always enlightens the intellect and sometimes touches the emotions, be a title to philosophical immortality, then McTaggart has fully earned his place among the immortals by the *Nature of Existence*.

It seems fitting, consequently, that this Memoir should conclude with some indication of McTaggart's achievements in his preferred and professional studies. The conspectus contained in these few pages is perforce inadequate, at best a pale reflection of the original, lacking not only the clarity and ease of its statement, but the force and cogency of its demonstrations, almost all of which are of necessity omitted. Under these limitations

I have tried to convey, in the first section, an impression of how McTaggart conceived the character and scope of metaphysical study, to show in what he believed its importance to consist and what kind of future he thought lay before it. The remaining sections are wholly occupied with an account of his own system; the second, with stating the conclusions he reaches about the formal character of what exists; the third, with what he claims to establish respecting appearance, error, their relations to reality, and ultimate value in the existent.

I

It is from a passionate interest in the great traditional problems of human nature and human destiny that McTaggart approaches the technical study of metaphysics. Its inspiration with him is emphatically a religious one. This, however, does not mean that its source lay in Christianity, nor in any other of what he calls "the traditional national religions". It is religious in the sense in which the inspiration of Plato, Spinoza, and Hegel—who accepted no such national religion—was religious; and again, in the meaning he defines as "an emotion resting on a conviction of a harmony between ourselves and the universe at large". Not that McTaggart affirmed, antecedently to investigation and proof, that there was such a harmony, but he was convinced that a denial of it no less than an affirmation was an issue of supreme importance to humanity, and one that could not be decided except by metaphysics. He conceived it, then, as a momentous matter, for his own sake and for the sake of his fellows, to discover whether a God exists; whether our will is free; whether we survive bodily death, and if so, to what end; whether the universe is more good than bad, and whether it becomes better or worse with the passage of time; whether what exists—the universe and ourselves in particular—has any purpose and value. Beliefs, affirmative or negative, on these questions, he was convinced, would continue to influence profoundly the happiness of mankind, with varying intensity at different periods of its history, by determining its attitude to reality:

It will depend on those beliefs, whether we shall consider the universe as determined by forces completely out of relation with the good, or whether, on the contrary, we may trust that the dearest ideals and aspirations of our own nature are realized, and far more than realized, in the ultimate reality. It will depend on them whether we can regard the troubles of the present, and the uncertainties of the future, with the feelings of a mouse towards a cat, or of a child towards its father. It will depend on them whether we look on our pleasures as episodes which will soon pass, or on our sorrows as delusions which will soon be dispelled. It will depend on them whether our lives seem to us worth living only as desperate efforts to make the best of an incurably bad business, or as the passage to a happiness that it has not entered into our hearts to conceive.

Are there any questions which affect our welfare more than these? It is true that what primarily affects our welfare is the truth on these matters and not our knowledge of the truth. But a belief that things are well with the world brings happiness, a belief that things are ill with the world brings misery. And this involves the intense practical importance of our belief on the problems of religion.

Now our hopes, our aspirations, our ideals, however passionate, however beneficent, give us no right to assert as true the dogmas on which they are based and without which they could not exist. Feeling may well set our problems, but never may it be permitted to solve them. Never are we entitled to believe a proposition because its truth would be very good or its falsity very bad.

There is no intrinsic *a priori* connexion between existence and goodness. If we can show that the nature of existence is such that it *is* good, so much the better. But then the question of the nature of existence is the one which we are setting out to determine, and we have no right to begin by assuming that that nature is good.

A religious attitude towards reality involves conviction concerning the truth of propositions of a certain sort. They are all propositions having what

McTaggart calls "metaphysical significance". That is, they are propositions whose truth—if they *are* true—is not disclosed by mere contemplation of their meaning, but by a systematic study of the ultimate nature of reality. For only by such an investigation can we hope to discover what that nature is, and whether it is such as to imply the truth of those propositions, or at least to render their truth probable. No man, therefore, is justified in a religious attitude except as a result of metaphysical investigation.

And this is a study that calls for many qualities—moral as well as intellectual—from the student. It calls for courage, since so much is at stake and because the delays, the obstacles, the forced countermarches, are many. It calls for faith, for in this study we must trust to reason and to nothing else, since the matter at issue is always one of proving or disproving something. And even when our proof is accomplished, still faith is required, to trust in the conclusions to which reason has brought us, especially "when they seem—as they often will seem—too good or too bad to be true", or else too strange and unplausible to be credible. Indeed, reason may bring us to conclusions that are in startling discrepancy with our ordinary beliefs. If a result seems highly improbable, we should suspend our assent and check our reasoning, to ascertain that no error lies undetected in it. But we may not doubt on inadequate grounds the conclusions to which reason has led us.

It is not, for example, right to doubt them because they surprise us very greatly, or because they appear to us paradoxical, or because they are incompatible with what had previously been regarded as certain. Nor, again, must we regard a conclusion with suspicion only because it makes the real state of the universe very different from its *primâ facie* state. The presumption, no doubt, is for the reality of what appears to be real, and we must not hold that the reality is different from the appearance until the difference has been proved. But there is no reason to doubt a line of argument because it reaches such a conclusion.

The importance of metaphysics, then, is plain, for much of it, in McTaggart's view, consists in investigating questions on the answers to which our dearest hopes depend. Nor have these practical effects on our lives been entirely overlooked in the past, though they have not always been sufficiently recognized. Few men limit their interests to their own quite immediate surroundings, and many men desire earnestly to know the truth about the ulti- mate purpose and prospects of their existence. If those who are not especially interested in these matters are a majority, those in whom present suffering does not create or awaken an interest are surely a minority. And are there not always some "who long for the truth with a longing as simple, as ultimate, as powerful, as the drunkard's longing for his wine, and the lover's longing for his be-loved? They will search because they must".

More often, however, it has been the practice to reproach metaphysics with being abstract and un-progressive, rather than with being occupied with what is unimportant. But in McTaggart's view it is precisely *non*-metaphysical questions which are, in comparison, abstract. Many of the difficulties peculiar to metaphysics arise just because the sub-ject is not more abstract than it is, and "if it pro-gresses more slowly than science, it is often because science, by its comparative abstraction, gains in ease and simplicity what it loses in absolute truth". Not that there is any conflict between metaphysics and science, once the vastly different character of their inquiries and their results is understood. But neither is any alliance between them possible. Philosophy, it is true, has been more or less domi-nated by some or other science at most periods of its history, and in McTaggart's opinion, the domi-nation has been on the whole more detrimental than beneficial to it. Again, consensus of opinion among experts, the general rule in natural science, but the rarest exception in metaphysics, is a direct consequence of the greater abstractness of science. Natural science has no right to pretend that its laws express the ultimate nature of reality, for it is powerless to justify the claim. Nor, indeed, does it assert so much, though popular thought usually supposes it to do so. Science affords no reason for believing that there are no laws of the universe more fundamental than its own, and of which its own are a manifestation. The assertion that there are no laws other than, or more fundamental than, those of physics, requires proof, no less than the contradictory assertion made by every non-materialistic philosophy. Both are assertions having metaphysical import, neither can be established or refuted by physical science.

McTaggart did not seek to minimize the amount of disagreement that exists on philosophical questions. But on religious dogmas and the tenability of the various traditional national religions the amount of disagreement, he pointed out, is much greater. Philosophy has doubtless advanced, but it has not done so by settling once for all one problem after another, so that there remains a constantly dwindling residuum. It has advanced rather by changing its *terrain*, and in consequence its progress is subtle and not obvious.

The questions evolve into different forms, but the answers are still various. We may hope that the long contest will eventually develop into a form where opposition will cease. But such a goal must at best be very distant, and many—though I cannot agree with them—fail to see any hope that it can ever be realized.

Indeed, McTaggart thought it quite possible that in time metaphysics would attain the same certainty in its sphere as the empirical sciences now enjoy in theirs.—"It would be rash to infer that metaphysics will never pass out of the controversial stage because they have not done so yet". And the possibility of eventual agreement on metaphysical questions presupposes of course that a future remains for metaphysical studies.

The study of metaphysics will perhaps never be very common, but it may be more common in the future than it is at present. The world's leisure is increasing, and much of it may be devoted to study. And if study at present is rarely study of metaphysics, that is largely because metaphysics seems unpractical. If, however, people find that they cannot have religion without it, then it will become of all studies the most practical. Its results, indeed, may not be more practically useful than those of some other subjects. For some results of study are, in our present civilization, essential to life, and life is a condition precedent of religion. But elsewhere we can enjoy the results without investigating them ourselves. I can eat bread, although I have never learnt to plough or bake. I can be cured of an illness, though I have never learnt medicine. But if— and this is the case at present—I have no right to rely on any metaphysical result which I have not myself investigated, then the study of metaphysics will be for many people the most momentous of all studies. And this may produce important results. For, after all, one great reason why so few people have reached metaphysical conclusions for themselves, is to be found in the fact that so few people have tried to reach them.

II

Mᶜ Taggart's last work[1], *The Nature of Existence*, is certainly his greatest achievement. But in spite of the extreme care in composition and perfect lucidity of expression, it is, in places, exceedingly difficult, and calls for sustained concentration to follow its close and complicated arguments. It is here Mᶜ Taggart's object to determine "the characteristics which belong to all that exists, or, again, which belong to Existence as a whole", and "to consider what consequences of theoretical or practical interest can be drawn from these general characteristics with respect to various parts of the existent which are known to us empirically". Now the problems raised by all beliefs "having metaphysical significance" (and therefore by religious beliefs) can be brought under one highly general question of the form: Is the nature of the existent such that so-and-so is true or false?—where "so-and-so" stands for the particular problem in question. Evidently then, in each case, an answer very largely depends on our having already discovered what *is* the nature of the existent. So the

[1] Mᶜ Taggart's other works comprise three brilliant and authoritative commentaries on the Hegelian philosophy: *Studies in the Hegelian Dialectic, Studies in the Hegelian Cosmology, A Commentary on Hegel's Logic* (Cambridge University Press), and a less technical work entitled *Some Dogmas of Religion* (London: Edward Arnold).

first of McTaggart's main and distinct undertakings is to demonstrate what must be the ultimate character of anything that exists, and hence the necessary formal structure of the totality of the existent.

It is desirable to begin by noticing the logical character of the method McTaggart employs and of the results it yields. The ideal is always absolute certainty, and even where absolute certainty seems antecedently unlikely, there would be no reason for abandoning the attempt to reach it until grounds were discovered showing why it should be unattainable. Now, *primâ facie*, three types of argument are open to McTaggart, namely, (i) *a priori* deduction, i.e., strict deduction from premises that are certain, and ultimately self-evident; (ii) deduction from premises obtained inductively; (iii) induction from experiential particulars. The last two methods, employed in everyday life and in the empirical sciences, may be called "inductive". Problematic induction is presupposed in both, and conclusions established by them can never be more than probable. *A priori* deduction alone can yield with certainty conclusions that are certain. This is the method McTaggart uses in his first inquiry, not only from preference, but because there is no other sort of argument that he could use in view of the peculiar nature of the problem. For here the possibility of proceeding inductively is ruled out from the beginning, since unlike deduction, induction requires to be justified by an appeal to ultimate facts about the universe, and therefore cannot be used, without circularity to establish what those facts are in character. Further, induction ultimately presupposes a class of instances that can be known empirically, but there can be no instances each of which is the totality of the existent.

With regard to the logical character of the results, the whole investigation may be divided into two extensive parts, the second requiring frequent resort to the facts of experience, the first being quite independent (except at one point) of all experiential information. McTaggart claims that the conclusions of the first part are demonstratively certain, that the negative conclusions of the second part (stating which apparent characteristics are *not* really possessed by the existent) are certain also, but that the positive conclusions of this part (stating which apparent characteristics *are* really possessed by the existent, and how these are related to the other, delusive ones) are not certain but still highly probable.

What, then, is the net result of McTaggart's first main inquiry? What are the conditions severally necessary and collectively sufficient to secure existence for what exists, or, otherwise, the conditions necessarily fulfilled by anything that exists?

Let us begin by getting clear about the most fundamental terms in McTaggart's system. These are existence, quality, substance and relation. Existence, which it is impossible to define but not difficult to identify, is a quality belonging to particular things or events, and, derivatively, to their characteristics. It is certain that this quality does find application, i.e., that something does exist. It is also certain that what exists must possess further qualities besides. There is no particular about which the whole truth is simply that it exists; an existent particular must be a particular *of some sort*; i.e., it must have some *nature*. And its nature, which includes its existence, consists of all the qualities that characterize it. Thus the nature of any existent particular is a compound quality, or, in other words, a quality analysable into parts that are qualities—simple or complex. Again, it is certain that the phrase "existent particular" has more than a single application, therefore, that there exists a plurality of particulars. Hence, relations in which these particulars stand, also must exist. Now the entities we are calling particulars, which possess qualities and stand in relations, but which are not themselves qualities or relations, McTaggart calls substances. (Most contemporary philosophers have abandoned the use of this term, though they cannot do other than recognize the existence of that for which McTaggart's term

stands. The phrase now usually employed to de-
note a substance is "a particular", where this is
opposed to "a universal". To indicate the latter
McTaggart uses the phrase "a characteristic", so
denoting either a quality or a relation.) The
quality of being a substance, then, unlike the
qualities of existing, of being a quality, of being a
relation, *is* definable. The definition defines one of
three ultimate types of entity that undoubtedly
exist and frequently require to be indicated. And
from this definition it follows that every particular,
whether its existence be of long or brief duration
(things, events, states, facts, groups of particulars,
classes of particulars), is a substance. Consequently
many things not usually called substances will now
be so called; e.g., a flash of light is a substance no
less than a mountain, the class of all coins is a
single substance, and each coin a further one, and
the group which consists of the flash, the mountain
and the class of coins will also be a single substance.
Thus, aggregates of substances in turn are substances, for they are neither qualities nor relations,
they do exist, and they have a nature different from
that of any of their parts. Every substance, then, is
qualified and related, for it stands in relations to
every other, as well as being related to each of
those relations in turn, and to each of the qualities
belonging to it. Further, every relation generates
in the terms it connects, the quality of standing in

that relation. These, "derivative qualities", form part of the nature of their substances, so were complete knowledge of the nature of any substance possible, we should know all that is true of that substance—all there is to know about it. It further follows that if one substance changes, all other substances must change.

On the basis of these results McTaggart establishes an extremely important principle, namely: that no two substances can have the same nature. Diversity (or numerical difference) without dissimilarity (or qualitative difference) is impossible. Among the qualities possessed by a substance, some are and some are not, directly generated by relations in which it stands to other substances. The latter are called "original qualities" of that substance, both together, its "primary qualities". Now the principle that the diverse is dissimilar must apply to the primary qualities of substances, but need not apply to their original qualities. Thus, the requirement of dissimilarity between substances is met by those differences among relational qualities that are engendered by differences among original relationships. Each substance is just the substance that it is because it has just the nature that it has: were that nature made different by the addition, withdrawal or substitution of any characteristic, then that nature could not be the nature of *this* substance, but of a numerically different one. Thus, even if the characteristic so conceived as added, withdrawn or substituted, does not intrinsically determine the remaining characteristics forming the nature of the substance, it does determine them extrinsically. So it follows that were one quality of any substance different from what it actually is, the whole universe would be different from what it actually is, for it would then not contain one substance that it actually does contain. Extrinsic determination thus holds between all the characteristics that are actually possessed by, and together make up, the peculiar nature of each substance. Intrinsic determination, however, holds between only certain characteristics, and not all of these need actually characterize any substance.

Again, it follows from the principle that the diverse is necessarily dissimilar, that every substance has an "exclusive description"—one that applies to it and to none other—by which it is absolutely identified. A "complete description" of a substance (i.e. a specification of all its infinite numbers of qualities, both primary and repeating) would, by the same principle, be an exclusive description of it. But an exclusive description need not be a complete description. Further, some descriptions are stated in terms of relational qualities of the substance described, and so necessarily refer to other substances. Hence, to identify a substance absolutely, it must be possible to replace such a description by another which specifies, not further substances, but only its own characteristics, i.e., by a "sufficient description". And from the fact that every substance must have an exclusive description, McTaggart claims to prove that it must have a sufficient one, although the cases in which we can *know* some given description to be a sufficient one, are few.

We have seen that a group of substances is a compound substance, that a group of groups of substances is a substance, and that every group generates an infinite number of repeating groups of each of which it is a part. Now the universe is a compound substance, for it satisfies the definition of substance and contains all other substances as its parts; but it is not a group, for it does not generate an infinite number of repeating groups, nor is it a class, for it has no members. There can be only one universe. Were there more, each would contain all existing content, but no two substances can have the same content. Hence the universe is distinguished from every other substance, and the phrase "*the* universe" is a sufficient description of it. Groups overlap one another in bewildering complexity. Of all the divisions disclosed throughout the length and breadth of the existent (divisions into groups, into groups of groups, into classes) no one is more fundamental than any other: all are

equally existent. And amid this network of reci-
procally determining natures and this complexity
of overlapping substances, only one fixed point has
yet been reached, namely, that substance of which
all other substances are parts, but which itself is
part of none—the universe.

This brings us to one of the most crucial and
difficult parts of McTaggart's system. There are
very many substances each of which is both a part
and a whole. But are there any of which this is not
true? McTaggart decides there are not, excepting
that substance which is the universe, and this,
though a whole, is part of no other whole. It is
self-evident, he claims, that every substance must
have parts within parts to infinity. Every substance
is thus endlessly divisible: none is simple. Now we
have seen that a substance must have a sufficient
description. But how can it be sufficiently described? One way would seem to be by furnishing
a sufficient description of all the members of any
set of its parts, but this, he shows, lead to a contradiction. For, a sufficient description of a set of
parts at one level in the series presupposes a
sufficient description of a set at a lower level, and
so on. But the series is unending, so we never reach
a lowest level. The presuppositions are therefore
never made good; no sufficient description of any
earlier level ever gets supplied, and since no set of
parts is ever sufficiently described, the substance of

which they are parts cannot be sufficiently described in terms of them. Yet every substance must have a sufficient description. Therefore it must be supplied in some other way.

There is only one condition under which the deadlock can be avoided. Therefore, since it is certain that a substance exists, and that the existent cannot be self-contradictory in its nature, this condition must be accepted, even though its truth is not intuitively or perceptively certifiable. The condition is—that there should be some one set of parts a sufficient description of which would determine sufficient description of all the lower sets. The parts of that particular set are called "primary parts" of the substance. But this condition depends for its fulfilment on a relation of a most complicated sort holding between the primary parts and their parts. This relation—one of "Determining Correspondence"—would have to obtain between one substance and part of another, and be such that a certain sufficient description of the former (specifying that it *is* in this relation to some or other part of the latter) intrinsically determines both a sufficient description of that part of the latter substance and sufficient descriptions of every member of a set of parts of *that* particular part of the latter substance, as well as of each member of a set of parts of each of *those* members, and so on *ad infinitum*. In this way, McTaggart claims to have

established that the universe must consist of a
certain range of substances (primary parts) which
are infinitely divisible, each into parts within parts,
where these parts are determined by determining
correspondence. If a substance exists, it must have
a sufficient description. It can have a sufficient
description if, and only if the theory of determining
correspondence is true. Substances *do* exist. Therefore, they are determined in this way. The universe
is a substance, therefore it is determined in this
way.

III

McTaggart's conclusions about the formal nature
of the universe and its contents are, to be sure,
astonishingly unlike that common view of its
nature based on, and inferred from, experience.
Not that his conclusions are obviously in downright
contradiction with this view of a world which contains material things in space and time, and ex-
periencing and acting persons, but rather that they
seem out of all relation with it. His second main
inquiry is therefore to discover whether all or some
of the more pervasive characteristics suggested by
experience *can*, and actually *do*, belong to any
existent. The presumption is in favour of experience; the assumption all through is that the existent really is as it appears to be, unless it is demonstrably otherwise. Accordingly, the inquiry

now assumes this form: Having regard to all that has been proved concerning the structure of existing content, is it such that some or all could be—temporal, material, sensal, spiritual, divine? Perception informs us that the first and either the second and third or the fourth of these characteristics at any rate *appear* to belong to every existent substance. But is it to substances, or only to their appearances, that these characteristics *really* belong?

Let us begin with time, for all our experiences seem to occur at, and to last through, some time. Time, as it appears, is analysable into two orders, the positions of each being related, respectively, as past-present-future (the "A series"), and as earlier-later (the "B series"). All occurrences we actually perceive appear as determined by both orders, and all past events remembered or inferred, as forming an A series. Now time implies change in relational qualities, for if one thing changes, *eo facto* everything else does too. But B-order positions are unalterable, earlier and later states of anything are eternal constituents of its nature. So the only characteristics that could change would be A-order ones. The A series, however, involves contradiction. For nothing can possess together the incompatible determinations of being past, present and future. Nor is the contradiction removed by saying that what *was* future *is now* present and *will be* past, for this starts an infinite regress that is vicious. Therefore, neither time nor change can be real characteristics of the existent, though they certainly are characteristics of the apparent.

McTaggart next considers matter, taken as that which possesses size, shape, position, mobility and impenetrability, with or without the usual "secondary" qualities. He has two independent arguments, one to show that the reasons commonly advanced on behalf of the reality of matter are quite inconclusive, the other to prove the *impossibility* of anything existent really being material. First, the support ordinarily alleged for believing in the existence of matter is a generalization of particular beliefs to the effect that this and that existent is material. Now never do we *perceive*, but always *infer* that "this" is a piece of matter. Although we do not *reach* beliefs in matter by inference, it is only by inference that these beliefs can be justified—if at all—namely, by showing that they are valid inferences from something we *do* perceive, i.e., sensa. But such inferences all assume the principle that the causes of the sensa resemble the sensa they cause, and this is something which experience assumes but cannot guarantee. Thus, so far as experience goes, the existence of matter "is a bare possibility to which it would be foolish to attach the least importance, since there is nothing to make it at all preferable to any other hypothesis, however wild". And, secondly, so far as metaphysics goes, McTaggart claims to have produced conclusive reasons for denying its existence, for none of the defining characteristics of matter, the spatial or the non-spatial ones, can satisfy the conditions of determining correspondence.

Likewise, the qualities of sensa cannot comply with the conditions of determining correspondence, therefore no substance can really be characterized by any of the qualities (e.g., colours, temperatures, tastes, etc.) with which we are acquainted through our senses. This, however, does not mean that when we seem to be perceiving sensa we are really perceiving nothing at all. What in fact we are then doing is misperceiving substances as having the nature of sensa, whereas really they have a different nature.

Can any substance be spiritual, i.e., have the nature peculiar to selves? To identify the quality in question is not difficult, for we each directly perceive it in perceiving one substance that possesses it—ourself. Doubtless much self-knowledge is knowledge by description, but this ultimately presupposes that the self described is also known by direct acquaintance. "Each self, then, who knows the meaning of 'I' (it is quite possible that many selves have not reached this knowledge) must do it by perceiving himself." Now the self with which each of us is acquainted has parts that are not selves though they are spiritual. Such parts are perceptions, awarenesses, judgments, assump-

tions, imagings, volitions and emotions. And of
these, it is argued, perceptions do, but awarenesses,
assumptions and judgments do not, satisfy the conditions of determining correspondence. All instances of imaging are really perceptions. Some of
these perceptions are erroneous and others genuine,
but all of them are misperceived in introspection as
being instances of imaging. Desires and emotions
are alike based on cognitions, for we cannot desire
without something being desired and without our
perceiving, judging or remembering what that
something is: nor can we fear or love without
knowing what it is that we fear or love. Desires
and emotions then are fundamentally perceptions,
though they are perceptions characterized by
unique and indefinable qualities. Some substances
therefore certainly do possess a spiritual nature.
Are there any which do not? To be sure, we cannot
experience or imagine a substance that is not
material or sensal or spiritual, and it has been
proved that none can be material or sensal. This,
however, does not prove rigidly that all substances
must be spiritual. Yet, since we cannot even imagine what another nature would be like, and since
it would have to be fundamentally analogous with
the nature of spirit (for, like spirituality, it would
have to conform to the conditions of determining
correspondence) it is reasonable to believe, and
unreasonable to disbelieve that all substances are

spiritual. Such a doctrine may be fairly called Idealism, but it is an Ontological, not an Epistemological Idealism.

Lastly, no substance can have a divine nature, i.e., there cannot exist a God—a personal being who is supreme and good, whether or not omnipotent and perfect. The universe itself could not be such a being, for a person cannot contain selves as parts. Nor could the universe contain one self which created all other selves, for creation involves the existence of something that did not exist before, and so assumes the reality of time.

So we see the second main inquiry culminates in four negative conclusions and one positive one. We may assert with certainty that no substance really exists in time, or really possesses the properties of matter, or those of sensa, or the defining characteristics of deity. We may assert—not with certainty but with confidence of high probability—that every substance is ultimately spiritual in nature.

Our present experience is, therefore, to a surprising extent, misperception. The existence of error is certain. Accordingly, it must be a genuine and important fact about the universe that it is so constituted that it *can* appear in these misleading ways,—its constitution must be compatible with the fact of erroneous perceptions. Consequently McTaggart's third main inquiry is concerned with showing that the formal specification of the ultimate nature of the universe, with which his first main inquiry terminated, does not preclude, but allows for, just those particular kinds of erroneous perception that are contained in present experience.[1]

Error is apparent but not unreal. Misperceptions really exist, for substances do appear as having natures different from those they ultimately possess. "Place, then, must be found for error", and, since it is always a perception that is erroneous, its only place can be in the percipient, not in that which is perceived. Now the types of error occurrent are limited in number, and since it is improbable that similar errors have dissimilar causes, it is probable that the causes of error too are few in number. Further, erroneous perception is highly differentiated, but differentiation in the determined can be explained only by differentiation in that which determines it. Hence, since all perceptions we introspect are perceived as being in time, the cause of erroneous perception (if it has

[1] Of McTaggart's attempt to show how the error in appearances is compatible with what he has established about the real nature of the existent, Broad writes: "Perhaps the finest part of the whole work is the transparent honesty with which McTaggart states and emphasises this problem, and the heroic effort which he makes to solve it in detail. Hegel brushes it aside with the magnificent epigram: '*Die Vollführung des unendlichen Zwecks ist so nur die Täuschung aufzuheben als ob er noch nicht vollführt sei*'; McTaggart accepted the spirit of this epigram and tried to show how it could be realized without contradiction".

a single cause) is probably connected with time. The problem for solution now is to discover the ultimate nature of that reality which is misperceived as conforming to the two time orders. Misperceptions that form an A-order must be erroneous perceptions of something that really is *not* temporal though it *is* serial. This reality is the "C series", all of whose terms are misperceptions (each being a member of a set of parts of a correct perception) having intensive magnitude, and differing *inter alia* in amount. In this way, we misperceive terms that are in a non-temporal series as being terms in a temporal one. Increments of difference in amount of perception are all characteristics of different perceptions of the same perceptum: "Nothing more must be perceived, but everything must be perceived more". (McTaggart admits the conception here is a difficult one: the imperfect analogy of seeing the same object now through a fog, now through a mist, may be helpful.) These different increments of perception possessed by various misperceptions in the non-temporal C series form in turn a further,—an "Inclusive" series, that is also non-temporal, namely the "D series".

At this juncture questions arise concerning value in the existent, and their treatment forms McTaggart's fourth and last inquiry. Time flows in an irreversible direction: changes occur in a forward,

not a backward, sense. From this fact certain very
important consequences for conduct ensue. Now
the fundamental direction—from earlier to later—
among events in the temporal B series, is correlated
with the fundamental direction—from lesser to
greater inclusiveness—among misperceptions in
the non-temporal C series. Of any two misperceptions, the one which is included in the other is
that which appears as occurring *before* the other.
And that term in the non-temporal series which is
thought of in the temporal one as the last, is the
term that includes all the others, but is itself included in none. This last term is a correct perception, but it is misperceived at all the pre-final
stages in the temporal series as being future. Since,
however, it is not perceived as in time, it can
never be perceived as being present or past. That
last term of the non-temporal series, then, appears
sub specie temporis as future, but not as transitory,
for it has no successor. Therefore it is naturally
thought of as an unending duration. This, the
popular conception of immortality as existence
through unending futurity, is our present misperception of our own non-temporal eternity. If
"immortality" means "having unending existence
in future time", then no self is immortal, for no
self is in time. If, on the other hand, "immortality"
means both "not ceasing to exist" and "*appearing
to exist throughout an endless future*", then every

self *is* immortal, for the only two conditions under which a self's existence could end are demonstrably impossible of fulfilment. The self's eternal existence, which appears as enduring throughout all time, implies pre-existence no less than post-existence. The self must have existed before the event appearing as the birth of its present body, and it will exist after what will appear as the death of this body. Now that which appears, *sub specie temporis*, as our present life is probably very short as compared with our life future and past. And this longer stretch of life is probably divided into many lives of which each is terminated by events that appear as births and deaths of different bodies. Even were the memory of each earlier life beyond recall in each later one, this would not destroy the self's identity. Memory is not lost, it is dormant. All memory recurs in the final stage of the non-temporal series, for this is a wholly inclusive and veridical perception of all the antecedent stages. The value of memory in our present life is that it helps to increase the wisdom, the virtue and the love in it. Just as acquirement of any skill does depend on past experiences but not on present memory of them—requiring rather that they should be forgotten—so "the value of love does not cease with the cessation of its memory". "The past is not preserved separately in memory, but it survives, concentrated and united, in the present".

Such a life as ours now, in which sin jostles with virtue, and doubt with confidence, and hatred with love, cannot satisfy us. But it can teach us a great deal —far more than can be learned between a single birth and a single death. Not only because the time is so short, but because there are so many things which are incompatible within a single life. No man can learn fully in one life the lesson of unbroken health and bodily sickness, of riches and of poverty, of study and action, of comradeship and of isolation, of defiance and of obedience, of virtue and of vice. And yet they are all so good to learn. Is it not worth much to be able to hope that what we have missed in one life may come to us in another? And though the way is long, it can be no more wearisome than a single life. For with death we leave behind us memory and old age and fatigue. We may die old, but we shall be born young. And death acquires a deeper and more gracious significance when we regard it as part of the continually recurring rhythm of progress—as inevitable, as natural, and as benevolent as sleep.

Good and evil are ultimate, indefinable values. Now the universe is a group of groups of selves. But value can attach only to selves that are members of groups, not to the groups. Therefore the universe has no value though there is value in it. True, certain states of a self determine the value of the self whose states they are, but the value does not belong to the states, nor, in strictness, to their qualities. The final stage of the non-temporal series is one of very great goodness as compared with the value of the present, for in it we have a complete perception of substances which now we perceive only incompletely. As we approach, *sub specie temporis*, to this final stage, there is a steady increase in the amount of perception, for every term in the series contains the amount of its predecessor and an addition. But, since the amount of those qualities which determine goodness may not increase regularly with the passage of time, the amount of goodness itself may not increase uniformly. The state of each self, however, does grow better as increase in the amount of perception increases, and such an increase does occur as we pass successively from earlier to later positions in time.

The more general characteristics of our experience in the final stage can be inferred with high probability. Since, in that stage, every part of a self is a correct cognition, there will be knowledge but no error. There may well be ignorance, for there are many substances which we do not now even misperceive or know indirectly. But such ignorance of substances is not, like error, an evil, though it is a limitation of the good. Some kind of emotion will be felt towards every substance we perceive in the final stage—"for other selves whom I perceive directly I shall feel love, for myself I shall feel self-reverence, for other selves whom I perceive indirectly I shall feel affection, and for the parts of all these selves I shall feel complacency". That love, besides being intenser, will be more

extensive: it will be felt for more persons then than
now. And love, unaccompanied, as it will be, by
unsatisfied volition, will yield pleasure. But the
pleasure need not exclude all pain. There will be
sympathetic pain felt for those now loved, on
account of the suffering that existed in their an-
terior lives. But we shall acquiesce in this evil as in
all else that really exists, and the acquiescence will
diminish, though not destroy, the intensity of the
pain felt in sympathy. Love, however, is not the
sole good. But it is the supreme good, for, once
it has passed a certain level of intensity, it is a
greater good than any that could arise from any
amount of knowledge, or virtue, or pleasure. But
although love is the greatest of all goods, it does
not follow that, even in the final stage, it will exist
in this supreme degree. The final stage will have
infinite value—that value will be infinitely greater
than the aggregate of values in the antecedent
stages, but this is a consequence, not of the love (or
any other quality) in it being infinitely intense, but
of it being unbounded. Further, this final acquiescence in the sin and pain of the antecedent
stages will be rationally justified and morally
virtuous, since it is necessary for the existence of a
supreme good, namely, a love that is intense and
passionate and eternal. Such love and the joy
accompanying it will infinitely outweigh the
sympathetic pain felt in that final stage. Mean-
while, until that stage appears no longer future, we

are powerless to limit the duration or the evil of the lives that must now appear as future:

There may await each of us, and perhaps await each of us in many different lives, delusions, crimes, suffering, hatreds, as great as or greater than any which we now know. All that we can say is that this evil, however great it may be, is only passing; that our lives are, with however much oscillation, gradually approximating to a final stage which they will some day reach; and that the final stage is one in which the good infinitely exceeds, not only any evil co-existent with it, but all the evil in the series by which it is attained, and thus the very greatness of the evil which we endure gives us some slight anticipation of the greatness of the good which outweighs it infinitely. Of the nature of that good we know something. We know that it is a timeless and endless state of love—love so direct, so intimate, and so powerful that even the deepest mystic rapture gives us but the slightest foretaste of its perfection. We know that we shall know nothing but our beloved, and those they love, and ourselves as loving them, and that only in this shall we seek and find satisfaction. Between the present and that fruition there stretches a future which may well need courage. For, while there will be in it much good, and increasing good, there must await us evils which we can now measure only by their infinite insignificance as compared with the final reward.

In timeless reality there is no change and no weariness, and that which is highest can exist without ceasing. What this would mean, even if the highest were no higher than it is now, it is useless to try to say except to those who do not need to be reminded of it.

CAMBRIDGE: PRINTED BY W. LEWIS, M.A., AT THE UNIVERSITY PRESS

For EU product safety concerns, contact us at Calle de José Abascal, 56–1°, 28003 Madrid, Spain or eugpsr@cambridge.org.

www.ingramcontent.com/pod-product-compliance
Ingram Content Group UK Ltd.
Pitfield, Milton Keynes, MK11 3LW, UK
UKHW012332130625
459647UK00009B/226